Prompt Engineering for Beginners

A Practical Guide to Communicating with AI

Kavya Iyer

8085 BOOKS

www.8085books.com

First Edition 2026

ISBN: 978-93-76066-148

8085 BOOKS

www.8085books.com

❖ Dedicated to ❖

Every learner, writer, and curious mind
who ever stared at a blank prompt box
and dared to ask a better question.

And to the engineers, researchers, and educators
who built these remarkable tools
and put them in our hands.

“

Clarity is not a constraint on creativity,
it is the language through which creativity
speaks to a machine.

Acknowledgements

Writing a book on a subject as fast moving as prompt engineering is never a solitary undertaking. Behind every page lies the curiosity, generosity, and shared knowledge of a remarkable number of people, and I am deeply grateful to each of them.

To the Prompting Community

My sincere thanks go to the global community of researchers, practitioners, educators, and everyday users whose questions, forum threads, blog posts, social media discussions, and shared experiments have collectively built one of the richest bodies of practical knowledge about working with AI models. This book is, in many ways, a distillation of that community's hard won wisdom. Every technique, every pattern, every cautionary example in these pages has roots in someone, somewhere, trying something and being generous enough to share what they learned.

To My Reviewers and Technical Experts

I am immensely grateful to the technical reviewers who read drafts of this manuscript with exacting attention. Their corrections, challenges, and suggestions improved every chapter. They pushed back where my reasoning was loose, flagged examples that did not quite work, and pointed out gaps that needed filling. Any errors that remain are entirely my own responsibility.

To the Editorial and Production Team

I want to thank the entire editorial, design, and production team responsible for shaping this book into its final form. Their professionalism, patience, and commitment to producing a volume that meets the highest standards of technical publishing transformed a manuscript into the book you are now holding.

To My Colleagues and Students

Over many years of teaching prompting techniques and applying them in professional settings, my colleagues and students have been my greatest teachers. Every question asked in a workshop, every confused look that signalled an unclear explanation, every workaround discovered under deadline pressure, and every moment of delight when a prompt finally clicked, all of it shaped the way the content in this book is structured and explained. This book is written for you.

To My Family

Finally, and most deeply, my gratitude goes to my family for their patience, encouragement, and understanding through the many evenings and weekends that writing this book demanded. Your support made all of it possible. Thank you for believing in the work, and in me.

Preface

Artificial intelligence has moved from research labs into everyday work in barely more than a few years. From the first conversational chatbots of the early 2020s to the powerful, multi modal AI assistants of today, the technology has remained on a steep upward curve, and yet the most important question it raises has stayed the same: how do we communicate with these systems effectively? This book is written to answer that question in depth.

Prompt engineering is the discipline of writing input that produces high quality output from an AI model. The name makes it sound technical and narrow, but the skill is broader and more human than the label suggests. At its core, prompting is communication. Every principle that makes a great prompt, clarity, specificity, audience awareness, structure, iteration, also makes great communication with humans. The tools change. The craft endures.

This book was written to be the single most useful prompt engineering resource a working professional or serious learner can own. It does not skim the surface of every technique, it goes deep into the patterns and practices that matter in real work. Every chapter is built around the question: how would a thoughtful practitioner actually use this? That question shapes the structure, the depth, the examples, and the practice exercises throughout.

The book progresses logically from first principles to advanced practice. The early chapters establish what prompts are and how they shape AI behavior, the foundations on which everything else is built. The middle chapters introduce structural patterns and core techniques, zero shot and few shot prompting, step by step reasoning, and iterative refinement. The later chapters extend into optimization, troubleshooting, and the design of reusable prompt systems that scale beyond individual prompts to entire workflows. The book closes with a reflection on prompting as a craft, a profession, and a way of thinking.

A note on scope: this book focuses on the universal principles of prompt engineering rather than the specific quirks of any single AI model. Models change frequently, and a book tied too closely to one vendor's product would be obsolete within months. The techniques in these pages have been verified to work across the major modern AI assistants, with notes where individual systems behave differently. The patterns themselves are the lasting asset. The model you use them with is a passing detail.

Whether you are picking up prompting for the first time, returning to it after early experiments left you frustrated, or moving into specialized areas like prompt chaining, retrieval augmented workflows, or team scale prompt libraries, this book is designed to take you further than you expected to go. The goal is not just to teach techniques. It is to develop the judgment that distinguishes a skilled prompt engineer from someone who merely knows how to type into a chat box.

How to Read This Book

If you are new to prompting, read straight through. Each chapter builds on the previous one. If you are experienced, skim Chapters 1 and 2, then dive into the techniques in Section 3 and the systems in Section 5. The optimization and troubleshooting chapters are useful at any level. Practice exercises at the end of each chapter are not optional, they are the bridge from reading to skill.

What Each Chapter Covers

This book is organized into five sections covering ten chapters, each building on the previous. The brief overviews below describe what each chapter contains and how it fits into the larger arc of the book.

Chapter 1: What Is a Prompt?

Establishes the foundational vocabulary. Defines prompts and distinguishes them from questions and instructions. Walks through the input output relationship that governs every interaction with an AI model. Compares weak prompts against strong ones to make the difference visible. Introduces the human analogy that grounds prompting as a form of communication rather than a technical specification.

Chapter 2: How Prompts Influence Output

Explores the mechanics of how prompt design shapes AI response. Covers the spectrum from clarity to ambiguity, the role of specificity, the importance of context, the influence of intent and expected outcome, and the most common mistakes beginners make. By the end of this chapter the reader sees prompts as levers, each word and structural choice influencing the output in measurable ways.

Chapter 3: Anatomy of a Strong Prompt

Breaks the strong prompt into its four building blocks: instruction, context, constraints, and output expectation. Shows how each block contributes to quality, how they combine in real prompts, and how to diagnose which block is missing when output disappoints. Provides worked examples that demonstrate the assembly of professional grade prompts.

Chapter 4: Prompt Design Patterns

Introduces the five core design patterns that cover the vast majority of professional prompting work: direct prompts, instruction based prompts, role based prompts, format driven prompts, and multi step prompts. Each pattern is explained, demonstrated, and compared against the others, with guidance on when to reach for each.

Chapter 5: Zero Shot and Few Shot Prompting

Covers the two foundational techniques every prompt engineer must master. Explains the mechanics of zero shot prompts that rely on the model's internal knowledge alone, and few shot prompts that use examples to teach the model custom patterns. Includes design principles for selecting the right number and shape of examples.

Chapter 6: Step by Step Prompting

Introduces the technique that turns the AI from a one shot responder into a guided reasoner. Explains decomposition, sequential prompts, scaffolded thinking, and the cognitive science behind why step by step output is consistently more accurate. Demonstrates the technique on tasks ranging from arithmetic to complex analysis.

Chapter 7: Iterative Prompting

Treats prompting as a feedback loop rather than a one shot transaction. Covers the iterative mindset, the diagnostic vocabulary needed to refine prompts efficiently, the patterns of follow up that produce the biggest gains, and the discipline of saving the final winning prompt for future reuse. Includes a real world walkthrough of an iteration session.

Chapter 8: Improving Prompt Quality

Focuses on the craft of elevating prompts beyond basic competence. Covers identification of weak prompts, reduction of vague language, control of tone and style, management of output length, and the precision creativity balance that defines professional output. Includes before and after examples that make the upgrade visible.

Chapter 9: Troubleshooting and Best Practices

A diagnostic and repair manual for the four most common failure modes: irrelevant outputs, incomplete answers, hallucinations, and inconsistency across attempts. Closes with a consolidated do's and don'ts list that captures the working habits of effective prompt writers across thousands of prompts.

Chapter 10: Building Reusable Prompt Systems

The final chapter steps back from individual prompts and looks at systems. Covers prompt templates, frameworks, structured approaches for different task categories, prompt library organization, and habits for scaling prompt usage in daily workflows. Closes with reflections on prompting as a craft, a profession, and a way of thinking.

About the Author

Kavya Iyer

Prompt Engineering Specialist • AI Workflow Consultant • Educator

Kavya Iyer is a professional prompt engineering specialist and technical educator with over a decade of experience designing, deploying, and training AI workflows across industries. Throughout a career spanning content operations, product development, knowledge management, and professional services, she has applied prompt engineering at every scale, from individual productivity tweaks to enterprise wide prompt libraries used by hundreds of practitioners.

Kavya Iyer has trained hundreds of professionals and learners in prompt engineering, from complete beginners to experienced practitioners seeking advanced skills in chained workflows, retrieval augmented prompting, and team scale prompt systems. Drawing on years of workshop and on the job training experience, she developed the teaching approach that defines this book: every concept is introduced in the context of how it is actually used in real work, not as an isolated technique demonstration.

A specialist in the integration of AI tools into professional workflows, Kavya Iyer has contributed to industry training curricula, presented at AI and design technology conferences, and written extensively on the application of prompt engineering to writing, analysis, software development, customer support, and creative work. Her practical orientation, every example tested in real conditions, every recommendation tied to outcomes that matter, runs through every page of this book.

Kavya Iyer is based in Bengaluru, India and continues to work at the intersection of professional practice and technical education. This is her first book on prompt engineering and AI assisted workflows.

Credentials	Areas of Expertise
Certified AI Practitioner (CAIP)	Prompt Design and Optimization
M.Sc. in Computer Science	Few Shot and Chain of Thought Techniques
Member, ACM India	Iterative Refinement and Diagnostics
10+ years professional practice	Prompt Library Architecture and Scaling
Speaker at industry conferences	Team Training and Workflow Integration

Table of Contents

Chapter 1: What Is a Prompt?

Before we can write better prompts, we have to be precise about what a prompt actually is. The word is now used so commonly that its meaning has become fuzzy. People say things like "I just typed in a prompt" or "the AI did not understand my prompt" without ever stopping to define what makes a sentence a prompt in the first place.

This chapter is the foundation of everything that follows. We will define a prompt with care, distinguish it from related ideas like questions and instructions, examine the input output relationship that lies at the heart of every interaction with AI, and walk through clear examples of what separates weak prompts from strong ones. By the end, you will have a working mental model that you can apply to every AI conversation you have from this point forward.

1.1 Definition and Role of Prompts in AI Interaction

At its simplest, a prompt is the text you provide to an AI model in order to receive a response. That definition, while technically correct, hides almost everything that matters. A more useful definition is this: a prompt is a structured piece of human communication, written in natural language, that conveys an intent, provides context, and signals desired output to an AI system.

Read that sentence again. Notice the four critical words inside it. Communication. Intent. Context. Output. Every effective prompt does all four of these things, even if you do not consciously notice it while writing one. Communication means the prompt is not just data, it is a message. Intent means the prompt has a purpose, a reason for being written. Context means the prompt provides background that shapes how the AI should interpret it. Output means the prompt has a destination, a desired result that the AI is expected to produce.

AI models, particularly large language models, are pattern recognition engines trained on enormous amounts of text. When you type a prompt, the model does not read it the way a human reads a letter. It processes the text as a sequence of tokens, predicting what tokens should come next based on patterns it has learned. The prompt is the seed that determines which patterns the model draws from. Change the seed and you change the pattern. Change the pattern and you change the response.

This is why prompts matter so much. The model itself is fixed. Its training is complete. The only variable you control is the prompt you give it. Everything else, the response, the tone, the structure, the depth, the accuracy, flows from that single input. In that sense, the prompt is the entire steering wheel of your interaction with AI.

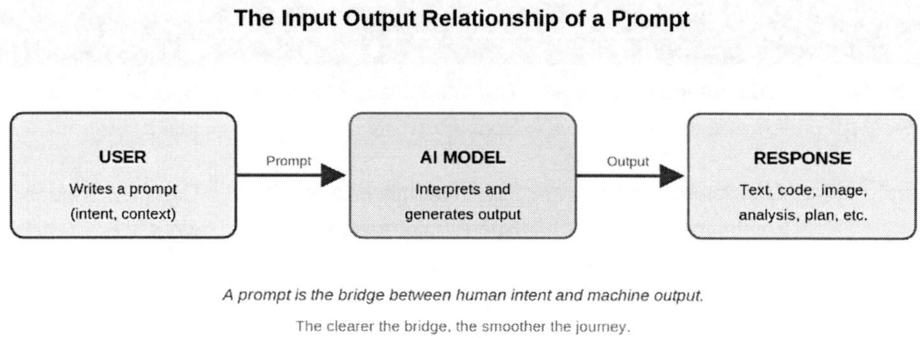

Figure 1.1: The fundamental input output relationship of a prompt.

The Role of the Prompt in the Larger AI System

It is helpful to zoom out and see where the prompt sits in the overall system. When you interact with an AI assistant through a chat interface, several things are happening behind the scenes. There is the user interface, which is the application you are typing into. There is the AI model itself, which is the trained system that generates responses. And in many modern systems, there is also a system prompt, which is a hidden set of instructions provided by the developers that shapes the model's behavior across all conversations. Your prompt sits on top of all of this, providing the specific request for the current conversation.

This layered structure means that your prompt is not the only signal the model receives, but it is the most directly controllable one. The system prompt and the model are fixed for any given session. Your prompt is what changes from one interaction to the next. Mastering the prompt is therefore the highest leverage skill in working with AI.

1.2 Prompt Versus Question Versus Instruction

People often use the words prompt, question, and instruction interchangeably. They are related, but they are not identical. Understanding the differences helps you choose the right approach for the right task.

Type	Definition	Example	Best For
Question	A direct query expecting a specific answer.	What is the capital of France?	Factual lookup, quick answers.

Type	Definition	Example	Best For
Instruction	A command telling the AI what to do.	Translate this paragraph to Spanish.	Specific, well defined tasks.
Prompt	A structured input combining intent, context, constraints, and desired format.	Translate this paragraph to Spanish, keeping the formal tone, and explain any cultural references in a footnote.	Complex or nuanced work.

Notice how the prompt in the third row contains the instruction from the second row, but adds layers. It specifies the formal tone. It asks for cultural references in a footnote. This is not just a longer instruction, it is a richer one. A prompt is, in many ways, a question or instruction with deliberate structure built around it.

Why does this distinction matter? Because the moment you start thinking of your input as a prompt rather than just a question, you start thinking about what supporting information the AI needs to do its best work. You stop asking only what you want and start describing how you want it. This shift in mindset is one of the single most valuable changes a beginner can make.

Mindset Shift

A question asks for an answer. An instruction asks for an action. A prompt asks for a deliberate, well shaped result. Aim for the third whenever the stakes are higher than a casual factual lookup.

1.3 The Input Output Relationship

Every interaction with an AI is a function. You provide an input. The system produces an output. In mathematics, a function takes some value and reliably transforms it into another. In AI, the same principle holds, but with a twist. The transformation is shaped by the input itself in ways that are not always obvious from the outside.

Consider a simple example. If you ask an AI to write a poem, you have given it an input. The output is a poem. But what kind of poem? A haiku, a sonnet, a free verse piece, a limerick, a romantic poem, a dark poem, a cheerful poem, a poem in English, a poem in another language? You did not say. The model has to decide. It will draw on the most common patterns in its training data, perhaps producing a generic short poem in free verse. That output is not wrong, but it is also not yours. It belongs to the average of every poem the model has ever seen.

If, instead, you say, write a four line cheerful poem about Monday mornings in the style of a children's book, the input is now richly specified. The output will be a poem with a specific length, mood, subject, and style. It will feel much more like your poem because you guided it there.

This is the core of the input output relationship. The richness of the output is bounded by the richness of the input. You cannot ask for something vague and expect something specific. You cannot ask for something specific without guiding the AI toward it. The relationship is not random. It is responsive.

How Inputs Shape Outputs

There are five primary ways in which an input shapes an output, and recognizing them helps you write prompts more deliberately.

1. Topic. The subject matter you specify becomes the central theme of the output. The more precise the topic, the more focused the output.
2. Format. The structure you request, whether a list, a paragraph, a table, or a script, determines how the AI organizes its response.
3. Tone. The emotional register you indicate, formal, casual, humorous, urgent, shapes the voice of the response.
4. Length. The amount of content you ask for, in words, sentences, paragraphs, or items, sets the depth and breadth of the output.
5. Audience. The reader or listener you describe influences vocabulary, examples, and complexity level.

Most beginners specify only the topic, and sometimes a hint of length. Skilled prompt writers consistently specify all five. The result is night and day different output quality.

1.4 Examples of Weak Versus Strong Prompts

Theory becomes useful only when grounded in examples. Below are several pairs of weak and strong prompts, with explanations of why each strong prompt outperforms its weaker sibling. As you read them, try to predict the kind of output each would produce, and then notice the dimensions along which the strong version improves.

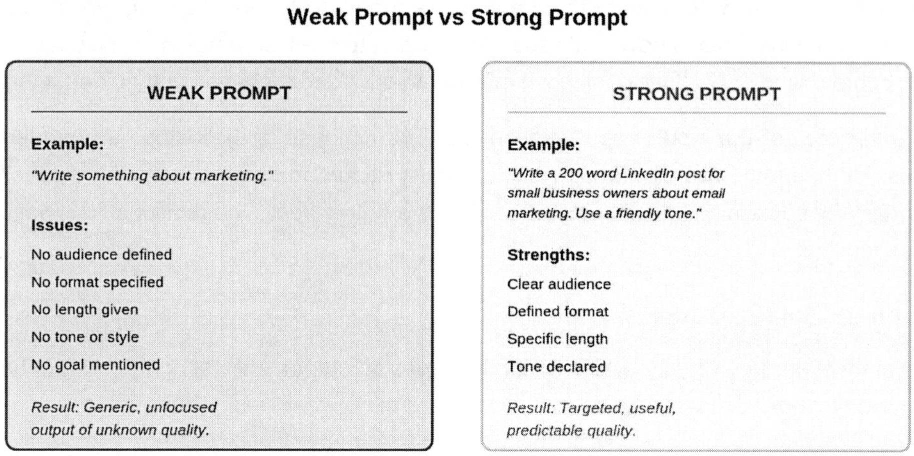

Figure 1.2: A side by side comparison of a weak prompt versus a strong prompt.

Example 1: Writing About a Topic

Weak prompt:

```
Write something about productivity.
```

Strong prompt:

```
Write a 300 word blog post for working professionals about three practical
productivity techniques they can apply during a busy workday. Use a friendly,
encouraging tone and include one short personal example for each technique.
```

The weak prompt leaves nearly every meaningful decision to the AI. What format? What length? What audience? What angle on productivity? The strong prompt answers all of these questions. The output will be measurably better, not because the AI is smarter, but because the AI now has enough information to be useful.

Example 2: Summarization

Weak prompt:

```
Summarize this article.
```

Strong prompt:

```
Summarize this article in five concise bullet points, each starting with a
strong action verb. Focus on the practical takeaways a small business owner
could apply this week. Limit each bullet to one sentence.
```

The weak version produces a summary, yes, but the AI has to invent its own structure, length, and emphasis. The strong version specifies the exact deliverable. There is far less room for the output to drift away from what you wanted.

Example 3: Code Help

Weak prompt:

```
Fix my Python code.
```

Strong prompt:

```
I have a Python function that should return the average of a list of numbers,
but it raises a ZeroDivisionError when given an empty list. Please review the
code below, identify the issue, and provide a corrected version with a brief
comment explaining the change.
```

The weak prompt does not even share the code, the error, or the goal. The strong prompt gives the AI everything it needs to provide a useful, targeted answer. Notice that the strong version is also more honest about what is broken, which makes the entire interaction more efficient.

Example 4: Creative Writing

Weak prompt:

```
Write a story.
```

Strong prompt:

```
Write a 400 word science fiction short story set on a remote space station. The
protagonist is a lonely engineer who discovers a strange signal. Use a
melancholic but hopeful tone. End with a question rather than a resolution.
```

The weak version is essentially a coin flip. You will get a story, but it could be anything. The strong version sets up creative constraints, and creative constraints are what make creative output feel intentional rather than random. The mood, the setting, the protagonist, the structural twist at the end, all of these guide the AI toward a story that actually feels like a story.

Example 5: Decision Help

Weak prompt:

```
Should I learn Python or JavaScript?
```

Strong prompt:

```
I am a marketing professional with no programming background. I want to start
automating repetitive data tasks like cleaning spreadsheets and pulling numbers
from reports. I have about 5 hours a week to learn. Should I start with Python
or JavaScript? Compare the two specifically for my situation in a short pros and
cons format, then give me a clear recommendation.
```

The weak prompt leaves the AI guessing about your context, your goals, and your constraints. It will produce a generic answer that could apply to anyone, which means it really applies to no one. The strong prompt gives the AI exactly the information it needs to give you advice tailored to your real situation.

> **Pattern to Notice**
>
> Every strong prompt above contains four ingredients: a clear task, relevant context, specific constraints, and an output format. The weak prompts contain only the task, and not always clearly. This pattern is not a coincidence. It is the recipe.

1.5 A Real Life Analogy: Giving Instructions to a Human

If you have ever managed a team, taught a class, mentored someone, or even asked a friend to pick up groceries on the way home, you already have intuition for how prompts work. The skills you use to communicate clearly with humans transfer almost directly to communicating with AI. The challenge is that we often write to AI in a way we would never speak to a person, and then we are surprised when the result is unsatisfactory.

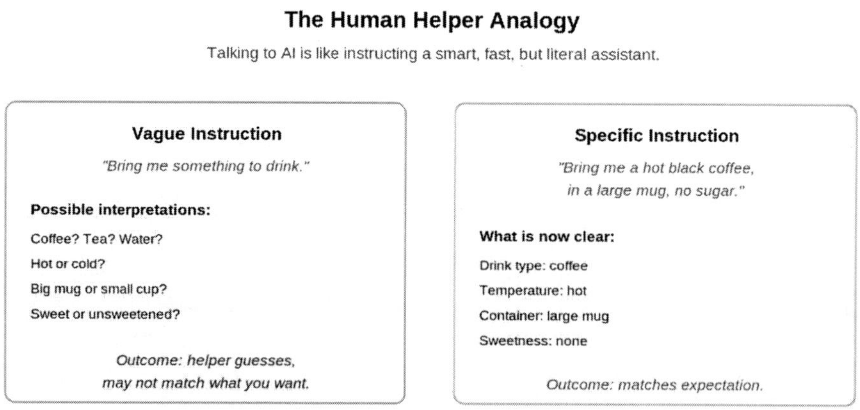

Figure 1.3: Vague instructions produce inconsistent results, whether the recipient is human or AI.

The Coffee Errand Analogy

Imagine you are at home, working on something important, and you ask a friend who is heading out, bring me back something to drink. Your friend is helpful, willing, and capable. But they are also a person, not a mind reader. They will return with something. It might be coffee. It might be tea. It might be a soda. It might be a bottle of water. They will guess based on what they think you usually want, what is convenient, what they themselves would pick. There is a real chance you will be disappointed, not because your friend failed, but because you did not give them enough information.

Now imagine you say instead, please bring me a hot black coffee, in a large cup, no sugar, from the bakery on Maple Street. There is no ambiguity. Your friend will return with exactly what you asked for. The act of being specific transformed a hopeful guess into a reliable outcome.

AI models work the same way. They are not adversaries. They are not lazy. They are willing helpers operating with whatever information you give them. If your instruction is vague, the output will reflect that vagueness. If your instruction is specific, the output will reflect that specificity. The AI does not punish you for being unclear. It just does its best with what it has.

The New Employee Analogy

Another useful way to think about prompting is to imagine you have just hired a new employee on their first day. They are smart and capable. They have read widely. They have done many similar tasks at previous jobs. But they have never been inside your specific company. They do not know your customers, your tone of voice, your internal acronyms, your style guide, or your priorities.

If, on day one, you say, write me an update for the executive team, the new hire will write something. It will be competent. It will look like an executive update. But it will not feel like your executive updates, because you have not told them what those look like. They will pick a generic structure, a generic tone, and a generic length. The result will be acceptable but forgettable.

If, instead, you say, here is an example of three executive updates we sent last month. Notice that they are always under 300 words, always start with a metric, always end with a single ask. Please write a new one for this week using the same structure, with these three updates as raw material, the result will be much closer to what you actually need. The AI, like the new hire, can do extraordinary work when given the context to do so.

> *Treat the AI like a brilliant new hire. It has the capability. It is missing only the context. Your prompt is the briefing.*

The Translation Analogy

A third helpful analogy is translation. When you ask a translator to translate a document, the quality of the translation depends not only on the translator's skill but also on the briefing you provide. Is this for a legal contract or a tourism brochure? Should the tone be formal or conversational? Are there any technical terms that should remain in the original language? Is there a glossary of preferred translations for company specific words?

A great translator working without context will produce a translation. It will be linguistically correct. But it may miss the spirit of the document, the intended audience, or the conventions of the field. A great translator working with a thorough briefing will produce something that feels native to its context, that lands the way the original lands. The same translator. Vastly different output. The difference is the input, the briefing, the prompt.

What These Analogies Teach Us

Across all three analogies, the same principle emerges. Capable helpers, whether human or artificial, deliver work in proportion to the quality of the brief they are given. The more thoughtfully you describe what you want, the closer the output will land to that target. This is not a quirk of AI. It is a universal principle of communication, and it is the heart of prompting.

1.6 Chapter Recap and Reflection

Let us pause and consolidate what we have covered in this chapter. Take a moment to reflect on each of these points before moving on.

- A prompt is a structured input that conveys intent, context, constraints, and desired output to an AI system.
- Prompts, questions, and instructions overlap, but a prompt is the most deliberate and structured of the three.
- The relationship between input and output is direct and responsive. Richer input produces richer output.
- Five dimensions consistently shape output quality: topic, format, tone, length, and audience.
- Strong prompts always include a clear task, relevant context, specific constraints, and an explicit output format.
- Communicating with AI is a lot like instructing a capable but uninformed helper. Specificity transforms outcomes.

Reflection Exercise

Before continuing to Chapter 2, work through these five steps. They are designed to convert what you read in this chapter into hands on practice.

1. Pick a task you have asked an AI to help with recently.
2. Write down the prompt you used, exactly as you typed it. Do not clean it up.
3. Using what you have learned, rewrite that prompt to specify topic, format, tone, length, and audience.
4. Run both prompts through your favorite AI tool, one after the other.
5. Compare the two outputs side by side. Notice not only how different the outputs are, but how different the experience of receiving them feels.

This single exercise, repeated a few times across different tasks, will accelerate your learning more than any amount of reading.

> **Key Takeaway from Chapter 1**
>
> A prompt is not just text. It is a deliberate act of communication that shapes what the AI can do for you. Treating prompts with care is the first and most important habit of effective AI use.

1.7 Deep Dive: How Models Process Your Prompt

To prompt well, it helps to have a working mental model of what happens between the moment you press send and the moment text begins streaming back. This section is not a technical computer science explanation. It is an intuition pump, a metaphor that captures enough of the truth to make your prompts better.

When you send a prompt to a modern AI system, the text is first broken into tokens. A token is roughly a chunk of text, often a whole word for common words and a sub word fragment for unusual words. The word water might be one token. The word antidisestablishmentarianism might be six. Punctuation marks are often tokens too. Spaces and newlines also matter. Every part of your prompt becomes a sequence of tokens, in order.

Once the prompt is tokenized, the model processes it through layers of statistical computation. At each layer, the model builds up a richer internal representation of the meaning, the relationships between words, and the patterns the prompt fits. This processing is not retrieval from a database. It is not lookup. It is more like the way a musician hears the first notes of a song and gradually builds a sense of what kind of song it is, what is likely to come next, and what would feel out of place. The model is doing this for your text, in milliseconds, with billions of parameters working together.

After the prompt is processed, the model begins generating its response one token at a time. For each new token, the model computes a probability distribution over all possible next tokens given everything that came before. It then samples from that distribution to pick the next token, appends it to the response, and repeats the process. This continues until the model decides the response is complete or hits a length limit. Every token in the response is influenced by every token that came before, including all of your prompt.

Why This Matters for Prompting

This mechanism has practical implications for how you write prompts. Because the model attends to every token in the prompt as it generates each response token, what you put in the prompt is reweighted continuously. Words that appear early establish context. Words that appear late often carry extra weight in the immediate next steps of generation. Patterns you establish, by examples or by structure, shape what the model expects to produce.

It also means that prompt order is not arbitrary. If you place your most important instructions deep in the middle of a long prompt, sandwiched between less critical material, those instructions may receive less effective attention than the same instructions placed at the start or end. A useful habit is to put your core ask near the start, provide supporting context in the middle, and restate the desired output expectation at the end. The double anchoring helps the model produce output that hews closely to your intent.

Token Budgets and Practical Limits

Each AI model has a token budget, the maximum number of tokens it can process across the prompt and response combined. Some models have small budgets, in the thousands of tokens. Others have large budgets, in the hundreds of thousands. Your prompt and the response together must fit within this budget. If your prompt is very long, less room remains for the response. If you want a long response, your prompt should leave room for it.

This budget is a constraint to be aware of, especially when working with long source material. If you paste a fifty page document into the prompt and ask for a comprehensive analysis, you may run out of room for the analysis. The fix is either to split the work across multiple prompts, summarize the source first and analyze the summary, or use a model with a larger token budget. Each option has trade offs. Understanding the constraint is the first step to working within it.

1.8 The History and Evolution of Prompting

Prompting did not appear suddenly with the release of conversational AI tools. It evolved over decades, drawing from earlier ideas in human computer interaction, command line interfaces, search engine queries, and natural language processing research. Knowing some of this history puts modern prompting in context and helps you appreciate what is genuinely new.

From Commands to Queries to Prompts

In the early days of computing, humans interacted with machines through commands. You typed exact instructions in a precise syntax, like list dot dash l, and the computer performed exactly what you asked. Mistakes in syntax produced errors. There was no interpretation. The command was the command. This style of interaction required learning the machine's language.

Search engines marked a shift. You typed words in your own language, and the engine tried to find the documents most likely to be relevant. The relationship became less about precise syntax and more about good keyword choice. You did not have to speak the machine's language. You did have to learn how to phrase questions in ways the engine could match. The skill of crafting effective search queries was an early ancestor of modern prompt writing.

Voice assistants pushed the relationship further. You could say full sentences. The system tried to understand intent. The output was often action, like setting a timer or playing a song, rather than text. The interaction was conversational but narrow, limited to the small set of tasks the system was designed to handle.

Modern conversational AI tools represent the next stage. You write prompts in fluent natural language. The system can handle an extraordinarily wide range of tasks, not just retrieval but creation, transformation, analysis, and reasoning. The richness of the interaction has expanded by orders of magnitude. So has the responsibility on the user to guide the system effectively. Prompting is the skill that meets this expanded surface area.

Lessons From the Lineage

Several lessons carry forward from this history. First, all of these interaction styles reward clarity. The clearer your communication with the machine, the more reliably you get what you want. Second, all of them reward a kind of empathy with the system. Knowing what kind of input the machine handles best helps you produce that kind of input. Third, all of them improve with practice. Crafting effective queries, voice commands, or prompts is a skill that compounds with use. Modern prompting is the latest expression of these enduring patterns, not a complete break from them.

1.9 The Spectrum of Prompting Skill

Across the people who work with AI tools, prompting skill is not a binary. It is a spectrum, with several recognizable levels of mastery. Knowing where you are on the spectrum helps you set realistic expectations and identify what to work on next.

Level	Behavior	Typical Output Quality
Casual user	Asks simple questions, uses short prompts, gives up if first try fails.	Generic, often disappointing for non trivial work.
Aware user	Knows that more context helps, sometimes specifies length or audience.	Decent for routine tasks, inconsistent for complex ones.
Skilled user	Routinely uses building blocks, iterates when needed, reaches for design patterns.	Reliably good output across most tasks.
Power user	Combines techniques fluidly, designs reusable templates, troubleshoots quickly.	Consistently excellent output, fast turnaround on complex work.
System builder	Designs prompt libraries, frameworks, and chained workflows for repeated use.	Produces leverage, not just output. Others benefit from their work.

Most people start as casual users and progress through aware to skilled with regular practice. The leap from skilled to power user requires deliberate study and accumulated experience with many different kinds of tasks. The leap to system builder is rarer and represents the application of prompting at organizational or team level. This book is designed to take you from wherever you are to the next level up, and to give you a path to system building if that is where you want to go.

Markers of Each Level

Casual users tend to write prompts that look like search queries or text messages. Their prompts are short, often missing context, and treated as one shot attempts. When the output disappoints, the conclusion is often that the AI is not as smart as the marketing suggests.

Aware users have learned that more context helps. They start to specify audience, length, or tone. They are willing to iterate, but the iteration is unsystematic, more like trial and error than deliberate refinement. Their output is noticeably better than casual users but still hit or miss.

Skilled users have internalized the building blocks, even if they could not always name them. Their prompts naturally include instruction, context, constraints, and output expectation. They iterate deliberately based on what the output reveals. They have developed a sense for which tasks need which kinds of structure. Their output is consistently usable across a wide range of work.

Power users go further. They have memorized several design patterns. They use few shot examples comfortably for unusual tasks. They break complex work into chains. They have a personal library of templates they reach for. They troubleshoot output problems with diagnostic precision rather than vague rewriting. Their output is not just usable. It is often excellent on the first try.

System builders apply all of this at the level of repeated processes. They design prompt systems that other people can use. They think about consistency across many runs, not just quality on a single run. They write documentation. They version their prompts. They treat prompts as infrastructure. This is the territory of teams and organizations as much as individual practitioners.

Where Are You?

Take a moment to honestly place yourself on the spectrum. Most readers who pick up a book like this are aware users moving toward skilled, or skilled users moving toward power. Wherever you are, this book is designed to help you take the next step. Knowing your starting point makes the journey clearer.

1.10 Twenty Real World Tasks Where Prompting Matters

Abstract principles become concrete when grounded in real tasks. Below is a survey of twenty common tasks that benefit dramatically from skilled prompting. As you read each, notice the kinds of decisions a strong prompt would make for that task and the kinds of mistakes a weak prompt would commit.

1. Drafting a professional email to a colleague you have a difficult relationship with. Strong prompts specify tone, intent, and the exact response you want from the colleague.
2. Summarizing a long meeting transcript for someone who was not there. Strong prompts specify length, structure, audience, and the kinds of items to highlight.
3. Generating creative names for a new product or feature. Strong prompts specify the brand voice, the target audience, the constraints on length, and the desired emotional register.
4. Writing a job description for a role you are hiring for. Strong prompts specify the seniority, the company stage, the team culture, and the kinds of candidates you most want to attract.
5. Analyzing a piece of feedback to identify themes and root causes. Strong prompts specify the categorical structure of the analysis and the granularity of the themes.
6. Drafting a difficult conversation script. Strong prompts specify the relationship, the goal, the emotional stakes, and the desired outcome.

7. Producing a comparison between two technical options for a non technical decision maker. Strong prompts specify the audience's literacy level and the criteria that matter to them.
8. Writing a product description for a marketing page. Strong prompts specify the brand voice, the audience, the call to action, and the length.
9. Creating a study plan for a topic you want to learn. Strong prompts specify your prior knowledge, your time budget, your learning style, and the desired depth of mastery.
10. Generating interview questions for a candidate. Strong prompts specify the role, the seniority, the qualities you want to assess, and the format of the interview.
11. Editing a piece of your own writing for clarity. Strong prompts specify what to preserve, what to change, and the standards for clarity.
12. Translating a document while respecting cultural context. Strong prompts specify the audience, the formality level, and any terms that should remain in the source language.
13. Brainstorming ideas for an upcoming project. Strong prompts specify the goal, the constraints, the desired number of ideas, and the kinds of variation you want to see.
14. Generating practice problems for a topic you are teaching. Strong prompts specify the difficulty level, the format, and the kinds of misconceptions the problems should target.
15. Drafting a personal story for a presentation. Strong prompts specify the audience, the takeaway, the emotional arc, and the length.
16. Creating an outline for a long document. Strong prompts specify the document type, the audience, the desired structure, and the kinds of sections that must appear.
17. Reviewing a piece of code for correctness and style. Strong prompts specify the language, the codebase conventions, the kinds of issues to flag, and the format of the review.
18. Designing a survey to learn about user behavior. Strong prompts specify the research question, the target respondent, the question types, and the survey length.
19. Writing a thank you note that feels personal rather than generic. Strong prompts specify the recipient, the relationship, the specific reason for thanks, and the desired tone.
20. Generating a list of objections a skeptical reader might raise about an argument. Strong prompts specify the argument, the kind of skeptic, and the desired depth of each objection.

Each of these tasks has a weak version that produces generic output and a strong version that produces output you can actually use. The skill of prompting is largely the skill of consistently choosing the strong version, even when the weak version would technically answer the request.

The Test of Real Tasks

If you cannot picture exactly how to write a strong prompt for these everyday tasks, you have plenty of room to grow. By the end of this book, every one of these tasks should feel solvable in a couple of minutes of prompt construction.

1.11 The Beginner's Bill of Rights

Before we move on to Chapter 2, here is a small charter for the reader who is just starting their prompting journey. Keep these ideas in mind as you practice. They will save you frustration and accelerate your progress.

- You have the right to be confused at first. Prompting feels strange because it is a new kind of communication. Confusion is normal.
- You have the right to expect the AI to behave in ways you did not anticipate. AI systems have quirks. Working with them includes accepting that you will sometimes be surprised.
- You have the right to not get a perfect response on the first try. Iteration is the norm, not the exception, even for skilled prompters.
- You have the right to ignore advice that does not work for your specific tasks. The principles in this book are grounded in many people's experience, but your tasks are yours. Adapt as needed.
- You have the right to use AI for tasks you find boring or tedious. There is no shame in delegating drudgery.
- You have the right to disagree with the AI and prefer your own ideas. The AI is a collaborator, not an authority.
- You have the right to ask the AI for help writing better prompts. Meta prompting is a real and useful technique.
- You have the right to enjoy the process. Prompting can be playful, creative, and rewarding. It does not have to feel like work.

Take these as permissions, not rules. They are reminders that this is a craft you are learning, and learning a craft has its own rhythms. You are allowed to be in process. You are allowed to grow.

1.12 Case Study Collection: First Encounters With AI

To make the abstract ideas of this chapter tangible, here are eight short case studies of real first encounters with AI tools. Each features a different person, a different task, and a different lesson. Read them slowly and notice what each person learned. The lessons compound.

Case Study 1: The Skeptical Manager

A regional sales manager named Theo had heard about AI tools but assumed they were marketing hype. His first attempt was to ask the AI to write a sales report for his region. He typed write a sales report. The output was a generic template with placeholder names and made up numbers. Theo concluded that the tools were useless and put off trying again for three months.

When he eventually returned, he tried again with a different approach. He pasted his actual numbers, named his actual reps, described what his manager wanted to see, and asked for a draft. The output was usable in a single attempt. Theo realized that what he had thought was an AI failure was actually a prompt failure. The AI was capable. He had not been giving it what it needed.

The lesson. The first impression people have of AI tools is often shaped by how they happened to prompt on day one. Many give up too early on tools that would have been transformative with a slightly different approach.

Case Study 2: The Overly Trusting Student

A graduate student named Amara used AI to draft sections of a literature review. The output looked authoritative. The references it cited looked real. She submitted the draft to her advisor, who immediately noticed that several of the cited papers did not exist. The references were plausible inventions, complete with author names, journal titles, and years.

Amara was mortified. She had not realized that AI tools could fabricate confidently. She rebuilt the literature review using only papers she had personally read, using AI only for stylistic editing rather than substantive content. The final review was strong, but the lesson stayed with her: confident output is not verified output.

The lesson. AI tools produce plausible content. Plausible is not the same as accurate. For any work where accuracy matters, verification is the writer's responsibility, not the AI's.

Case Study 3: The Iterative Designer

A freelance graphic designer named Pavel used AI to write copy for client projects. His first attempts produced generic copy that did not match any specific brand. He noticed that he was iterating five or six times for each project, getting frustrated each time.

After a month of this, Pavel started saving the prompts that produced strong copy. He noted what made each one work: specific brand voice descriptions, audience information, examples of copy he liked. Within three months, he had a small library of prompt templates organized by industry. New projects took half as long because the templates did most of the work.

The lesson. The skilled prompt writer treats prompts as assets, not as disposable text. Saving and refining your best prompts is one of the highest leverage habits in this practice.

Case Study 4: The Medical Resident

A medical resident named Yuki tried using AI to study for her board exams. Her first attempts produced clear summaries of medical concepts. But she noticed that occasionally the AI would state something subtly wrong, like a misnamed dosage or an outdated guideline. The information sounded right, but it was not always right.

Yuki adjusted her approach. She used the AI to organize study material she sourced from authoritative texts, rather than to produce medical knowledge from scratch. She would paste a chapter from her textbook and ask for summaries, comparisons, or quiz questions based on the source. The AI was excellent at structuring information she trusted, but unreliable as a primary source.

The lesson. AI is a great tool for working with information, but a risky source of information. Especially in domains where accuracy is critical, treat the AI as a structuring tool, not a knowledge base.

Case Study 5: The Storyteller

A novelist named Camille used AI to brainstorm story ideas. Her first prompts produced generic story premises that felt like every other AI generated story she had seen. She kept iterating, becoming frustrated.

Then she changed her approach. Instead of asking for ideas in a vacuum, she described her own writing voice, her favorite themes, the kinds of characters she wrote, and the emotional registers she preferred. The AI began producing ideas that felt like they could be hers. She was using the AI to amplify her own taste rather than to substitute for it.

The lesson. AI works best as an extension of you, not a replacement for you. The more it knows about your preferences, your context, and your taste, the more useful it becomes.

Case Study 6: The Career Switcher

A man named Garrett was changing careers from finance to user experience design. He used AI to learn the new field. His first prompts asked for explanations of UX concepts. The output was helpful but generic, like reading any introductory article.

He realized he could ask better questions. He started prompting with phrases like I am a former finance professional learning UX. Explain heuristic evaluation in a way that draws on what someone with my background would already understand. The output transformed. The AI used analogies from finance, mapped UX concepts to investment frameworks Garrett already knew, and produced explanations that felt personally tailored.

The lesson. Telling the AI who you are and what you bring transforms its output. It is not a search engine returning generic articles. It is a tutor that adapts to its student.

Case Study 7: The Anxious First Timer

A retired teacher named Olive felt anxious about using AI. She worried she would do something wrong or break something. Her first prompts were tentative and apologetic, like sorry to bother you, could you possibly tell me a little about gardening if it is not too much trouble. The output was polite but unfocused.

Her granddaughter showed her that the AI did not need to be coddled. Olive learned to write direct, specific prompts. The AI's output became dramatically more useful. Olive realized that she had been treating the AI like a stranger she did not want to inconvenience, when it was more like a willing colleague waiting for clear direction.

The lesson. The AI does not need pleasantries. It needs direction. Beginners often imagine that being polite produces better output. The opposite is closer to true: being clear and specific produces better output. Politeness in prompts is a habit you can drop without consequence.

Case Study 8: The Power User

A product manager named Kai had been using AI for two years and had a library of seventy templates. She knew most of the techniques in this book. Yet she still encountered prompts that did not work the way she expected. She had developed a habit of treating each unexpected output as a puzzle. What about my prompt led to this output? What change would have produced what I wanted? Each puzzle solved made her a slightly better prompt writer.

After two years, Kai had quietly become one of the most effective AI users in her company. New colleagues asked her for help. Her library was shared widely. Her practice was the result of two years of small, consistent effort, not a sudden burst of mastery.

The lesson. Mastery in prompting is the cumulative result of curiosity sustained over time. There are no shortcuts, but there are no obstacles either. Every day you practice, you get a little better.

1.13 The Underlying Mental Model: How to Think About Prompts

Beyond techniques, there is a mental model that distinguishes effective prompt writers. The model has three parts. First, prompts are not commands but instructions to a collaborator. The AI is not executing code; it is interpreting language. Second, prompts must carry their own context. The AI cannot read your mind, your screen, your history, or your team's conventions unless you bring those into the prompt. Third, prompts produce output through a kind of pattern matching against vast training experience. The patterns you invoke through your phrasing shape what comes back.

This mental model has practical implications. Treating the AI as a collaborator means being clear about what you want, providing the context the collaborator needs, and being willing to clarify when the first attempt does not land. Treating prompts as context carriers means including the audience, situation, and reference material in the prompt itself. Treating output as pattern matching means writing prompts that invoke the patterns you want, rather than expecting the AI to generate from scratch.

Hold this model loosely. It is a working approximation, not a complete description of how AI systems function. But it is a useful approximation, and it produces better prompts than any technical or theoretical model. The collaborator metaphor, though imperfect, gets the most important things right.

1.14 Reflective Exercises

To help the ideas in this chapter settle, here are several reflective exercises. Try them in writing or in conversation with someone who works with AI.

1. Describe in your own words what a prompt is, without using any of the language from this chapter.
2. Recall a time when an AI output disappointed you. With hindsight, what was missing from your prompt that would have produced better output?
3. Recall a time when an AI output exceeded your expectations. What about your prompt do you think contributed to that success?
4. List three tasks in your work or life where you think AI could help, and for each, write a sample prompt you would try first.
5. If you were teaching prompting to a friend, what is the single most important idea you would want them to take away from chapter one?

These exercises are not tests. They are mirrors. They show you what you actually believe about prompting, which is more important than what any book tells you to believe. The clearer your own understanding, the more reliably you can apply it under pressure.

1.15 Common Misconceptions Cleared Up

Beginners often arrive with misconceptions that quietly limit their progress. Below are eight common misconceptions, each addressed directly.

Misconception 1: AI Tools Have Hidden Magic Words

Some beginners believe that there are special phrases or magic words that unlock superior performance. There are not. Output quality comes from clarity, specificity, context, and structure, not from secret incantations. Phrases like let us think step by step or you are an expert can help in specific contexts, but they are not magic. They are reminders to the AI of useful patterns.

Misconception 2: Longer Prompts Are Always Better

Length matters, but quality matters more. A focused 100 word prompt with the right context can outperform a 500 word prompt full of noise. Add length only when each addition contributes meaningfully. Padding does not help.

Misconception 3: The AI Knows What You Mean

It does not. The AI knows only what is in the prompt. Anything you assume but do not state, the AI must guess. The guessing is often wrong. Make your assumptions explicit.

Misconception 4: One Try Is Enough

Most successful prompts come from iteration. The first attempt is rarely the best. Treat the first output as a starting point, not a finished product.

Misconception 5: The AI Is Always Confident, So It Is Always Right

AI tools produce confident sounding text by training. Confidence is a stylistic feature, not a measure of accuracy. Always evaluate output on substance, especially for factual content.

Misconception 6: Politeness Helps

It does not measurably help. The AI does not need please or thank you to produce better output. Spend your prompt on direction, not pleasantries.

Misconception 7: The AI Has Memory of Past Conversations

In most consumer interfaces, it does not. Each conversation is independent. Even within a conversation, the AI's memory is limited to what fits in the context window. Bring the context the AI needs into each conversation.

Misconception 8: AI Is Replacing Human Skill

AI is amplifying human skill, not replacing it. The bottleneck has shifted from execution to direction. The skill of directing AI well is the new lever. People who learn this skill have more leverage than those who do not. Skill remains essential. The skill has just changed.

1.16 The Inner Practice

So far, we have focused on what to do when prompting. Beneath the doing is an inner practice, a set of attitudes and habits of mind that shape how you approach every prompt. This inner practice is harder to teach but possibly more important than any specific technique.

Curiosity About Output

The skilled prompter is genuinely curious about what the AI produces. They read each output carefully. They ask why it took the shape it did. They notice the patterns the AI fell into and the patterns it avoided. This curiosity sustains learning across thousands of interactions. Without it, prompting becomes mechanical, and improvement plateaus.

Patience With Iteration

The skilled prompter does not expect the first try to be the best. They iterate calmly, treating each attempt as data rather than failure. The patience compounds. Many prompt writers fail to develop because they stop after the first attempt and conclude the AI cannot do what they want.

Humility About Limitations

The skilled prompter knows the AI's limits. They do not ask it to do things it cannot do well. They verify when accuracy matters. They keep their expectations calibrated to actual capability. This humility prevents disappointment and produces realistic output.

Generosity Toward the AI

The skilled prompter provides the AI with what it needs. Context. Examples. Constraints. The provision is generous. They do not expect the AI to read their mind. They make their expectations explicit. This generosity flows back as better output.

Discipline About Documentation

The skilled prompter saves what works. They build their library. They tag their templates. They document when each is useful. This discipline produces compounding returns over months and years. It is the boring habit that separates advanced practitioners from beginners more than any technique.

The Inner Game

Techniques are the outer game. Curiosity, patience, humility, generosity, and discipline are the inner game. The outer game without the inner game produces mechanical prompting. The inner game without the outer game produces sympathetic but ineffective prompting. Together they produce mastery.

Chapter 2: How Prompts Influence Output

In Chapter 1, we established that prompts shape outputs. That is the principle. In this chapter, we examine the mechanics. How exactly does a prompt influence what the AI produces? What specific aspects of a prompt matter most? And what are the common mistakes that beginners make, often without realizing it, that produce unsatisfying results?

Understanding the mechanics matters because it turns prompting from guesswork into engineering. Once you can see why a prompt is producing a certain kind of output, you can change the prompt deliberately to produce a different kind of output. Without this understanding, prompting feels like luck. With it, prompting becomes a skill you can improve consistently over time.

2.1 Clarity Versus Ambiguity in Prompts

Clarity is the single most important property of an effective prompt. By clarity, we mean that the prompt can be interpreted in only one reasonable way. Ambiguity, by contrast, occurs when a prompt can be interpreted in multiple ways, leaving the AI to choose between them. The AI will choose, but it may not choose what you intended.

Consider the prompt, write a short article about apples. The word apples is ambiguous. Are we talking about the fruit, the technology company, or some other meaning? The word short is ambiguous. Does it mean 100 words, 500 words, or two paragraphs? The word article is ambiguous. Does it mean a news article, a blog post, an academic paper, or a casual write up? Each of these ambiguities forces the AI to make a guess. The combined effect of multiple guesses is unpredictable output.

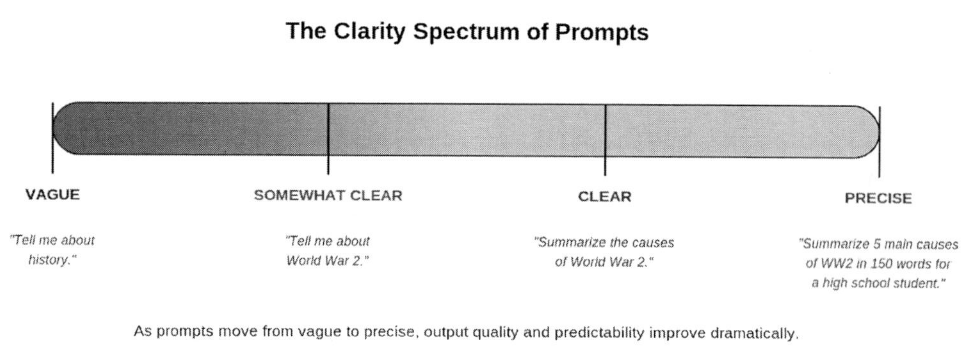

Figure 2.1: Prompts exist on a spectrum from vague to precise. Output quality follows the same curve.

Sources of Ambiguity

Ambiguity creeps into prompts in several recognizable ways. Becoming aware of these sources is the first step toward eliminating them.

Source	Example	Why It Confuses
Vague nouns	"the document," "the file," "the topic"	AI may not know which document or topic you mean.
Vague verbs	"improve," "fix," "clean up"	Improve along which dimension? Fix what aspect?
Vague adjectives	"good," "better," "professional"	Subjective terms with no shared definition.
Implicit context	"As we discussed earlier..."	AI may not have access to that earlier context.
Mixed signals	"Be brief but thorough"	These goals can conflict and confuse the model.
Pronouns without antecedents	"Make it shorter."	What is "It"?

Notice that ambiguity is rarely a single dramatic problem. It is usually a series of small fuzzy spots that compound together. A prompt with one vague word might still produce decent output. A prompt with five vague words is rolling dice.

How to Increase Clarity

Increasing clarity is a matter of replacing vague terms with specific ones. Rather than say good, say accurate and well organized. Rather than say short, say in 200 words or fewer. Rather than say improve, say rewrite to be more concise while keeping the original meaning. Each replacement removes a guess that the AI would otherwise have to make on your behalf.

There is a useful test you can apply. After writing a prompt, read it back as if you were a stranger. Could you misinterpret any part of it? Could a reasonable person produce a different output than what you intended? If yes, refine those parts. This habit, applied consistently, transforms the way you write prompts.

Clarity Self Test

After writing a prompt, ask yourself, if I gave this exact prompt to ten different people, would they produce roughly the same output? If yes, your prompt is clear. If no, identify which parts of the prompt are causing the divergence and tighten them.

2.2 Specificity and Detail Level

Specificity is closely related to clarity, but not identical. A prompt can be clear and still lack specificity. For example, the prompt write a 200 word essay about climate change is clear. There is no ambiguity. But it is not specific. Climate change is an enormous topic. The AI has to choose which angle to take, which aspects to cover, which audience to write for. Adding specificity narrows the focus.

A more specific version might be, write a 200 word essay for a high school student explaining how rising global temperatures affect ocean ecosystems. Use simple vocabulary and include one concrete example. Now the AI knows the topic, the audience, the angle, the vocabulary level, and even a structural requirement. The result will be measurably better aligned with what you actually wanted.

Levels of Detail

Specificity is not all or nothing. It exists on a scale. The right level of detail for a prompt depends on the task. A simple task may not need much specification. A complex task often benefits from a great deal. The skill lies in matching the level of detail to the requirements of the situation.

Task Complexity	Recommended Detail Level	Example
Casual lookup	Minimal	What year was the Eiffel Tower built?
Quick assistance	Moderate	Give me three meal ideas using chicken, rice, and broccoli.
Deliverable creation	High	Draft a 250 word LinkedIn post about remote team rituals, written in a warm conversational tone, ending with an open question.
Strategic or sensitive work	Very high	Full briefing including audience, goals, constraints, examples, and edge cases.

There is a temptation to think that more detail is always better. It is not. Over specification can also harm a prompt by introducing contradictions, overwhelming the AI with constraints, or stripping out the creative latitude that makes the output interesting. The goal is not maximum detail. The goal is sufficient detail. Sufficient means enough that the AI can do the work well, but not so much that the prompt becomes brittle.

The Just Enough Principle

A useful guideline is what we will call the just enough principle. Add detail to a prompt as long as each addition meaningfully improves the output. Stop adding detail when further additions either fail to change the output or actively make it worse. This principle is best learned through practice. Run the same task with prompts of escalating detail. Notice the moment when more detail stops helping. That is your zone for that kind of task.

2.3 Context Setting Basics

Context is the background information that helps the AI interpret your prompt correctly. Without context, the AI must rely on its general training data. With context, it can tailor its response to your specific situation. Setting context well is one of the most powerful skills in prompting, and one of the most consistently underused.

Context can take many forms. It can be background information about you. It can be background information about the audience for the output. It can be examples of the kind of output you want. It can be data, files, or text that the AI should reference. It can be constraints from your environment that shape what is possible. Each of these forms of context helps the AI position its response correctly.

Five Categories of Context

Category	What It Provides	Example
Personal	Who you are, your role, your expertise level.	I am a beginner to financial planning.
Audience	Who the output is for.	This will be read by senior executives.
Situational	What is happening that prompted the request.	We just lost a major client and need to rebuild trust.

Category	What It Provides	Example
Reference	Source material the AI should use or respect.	Here is the email I am responding to...
Stylistic	Tone, voice, and formatting preferences.	Match the tone of the example provided below.

A prompt that uses all five categories will produce dramatically more relevant output than a prompt that uses none. But not every prompt needs all five. The categories are tools to reach for, not boxes to check. As you write more prompts, you will develop instincts for which categories matter most for which kinds of tasks.

How Much Context Is Too Much?

There is a balance to strike. Too little context produces generic output. Too much context produces bloated prompts that are hard to maintain and may dilute the most important information. The skill is to include the context that is genuinely relevant to the task and leave out the context that is not.

A simple test, when reading a context block of your prompt, ask yourself, would removing this sentence change the output the AI produces? If yes, keep it. If no, consider removing it. This pruning process, applied systematically, produces prompts that are dense with useful information and free of filler.

> *Context is the difference between an answer and the right answer. The AI cannot give you what fits your situation if it does not know what your situation is.*

2.4 Prompt Intent and Expected Outcome

Every prompt has an intent, a reason it was written. Sometimes that intent is obvious from the prompt itself. Often it is implicit, sitting in the writer's head but never appearing in the text. When intent is implicit, the AI must guess at it. When intent is explicit, the AI can serve it directly.

Stating intent explicitly is a small change with outsized effects. Compare these two prompts.

```
Summarize the attached meeting notes.
```

```
Summarize the attached meeting notes. The summary will be sent to team members
who could not attend, so it should highlight key decisions and any action items
assigned to specific people.
```

The first prompt produces a summary. The second produces a summary that is fit for purpose. The intent, communicating with absent team members, shapes the choices the AI makes about what to include and what to leave out. Decisions and action items rise to the top. Tangential discussion gets compressed or dropped.

Expected Outcome as a Steering Mechanism

Closely related to intent is expected outcome. While intent answers the question why am I asking, expected outcome answers the question what should the response look like. The two work together. Intent shapes the substance of the output. Expected outcome shapes its form.

If you say, the result should be a single paragraph that I can paste into an email, you have given the AI a clear destination. It will not produce a long list with subheadings, because that does not match the expected outcome. It will produce a clean paragraph. The AI is not trying to win a competition for the most elaborate response. It is trying to give you what you said you needed. Telling it what you need is therefore a powerful steering tool.

The Why and What Pair

In practice, including both why and what at the start of a prompt is one of the simplest ways to dramatically improve output. The why provides intent. The what provides expected outcome. Together, they orient the entire response.

> **Practical Pattern**
>
> Open complex prompts with two short sentences. The first describes why you want the output. The second describes what the output should look like. After that, add the rest of the task. This pattern alone can transform mediocre prompts into excellent ones.

2.5 Common Beginner Mistakes

As you start writing more prompts, you will likely encounter the same recurring problems that almost every beginner faces. Knowing the patterns in advance helps you avoid them, or at least recognize them quickly when they appear. We will walk through the eight most common mistakes, with examples and corrections.

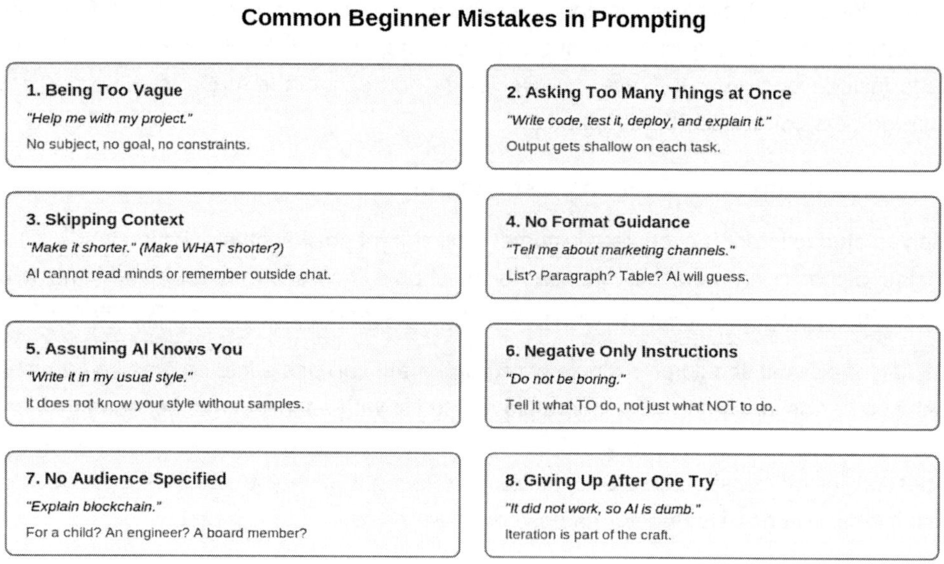

Figure 2.2: A field guide to the most common beginner mistakes in prompt writing.

Mistake 1: Being Too Vague

By far the most common mistake is writing prompts that are too vague. Help me with my project. Make this better. Tell me about technology. These prompts feel like requests, but they do not give the AI enough to work with. The cure is to specify the subject, the goal, and at least one constraint. Even a small amount of specificity dramatically improves results.

Mistake 2: Asking Too Many Things at Once

Beginners often try to pack many tasks into a single prompt. Write the code, then test it, then explain it, then suggest improvements, then write a tutorial. The AI will attempt all of them, but each task will receive shallow attention. Better to break the work into separate prompts, addressing each task in depth before moving to the next. Chapter 6 discusses step by step prompting in detail.

Mistake 3: Skipping Context

This mistake takes many forms. Sometimes the user assumes the AI remembers earlier conversations it cannot access. Sometimes they refer to a document the AI has not seen. Sometimes they say make it shorter without specifying what it refers to. The cure is to include all the context the AI needs within the prompt itself, even if it feels redundant.

Mistake 4: No Format Guidance

If you do not specify the format, the AI will pick one, and it may not be the one you wanted. A request for marketing channel ideas might come back as a list, a paragraph, a table, or a casual essay. If you wanted a specific format, say so. List, table, bullet points, paragraph, JSON, all of these are valid choices. Be explicit.

Mistake 5: Assuming the AI Knows You

Phrases like in my usual style, the way I always do it, or like the last one only work if the AI has seen examples. It does not have memory of you outside the current conversation in most cases. The cure is to provide examples or descriptions of your style instead of relying on assumed knowledge.

Mistake 6: Negative Only Instructions

Telling the AI what not to do is far less effective than telling it what to do. Do not be boring leaves the AI with no positive direction. Use vivid language and concrete examples gives it something to aim for. Whenever you find yourself writing a do not, ask whether you can replace it with a do. Positive guidance is almost always more effective.

Mistake 7: No Audience Specified

Different audiences require different language, examples, and depth. A prompt that says explain blockchain produces a generic explanation. A prompt that says explain blockchain to a curious eleven year old produces a kid friendly explanation with relatable analogies. A prompt that says explain blockchain to a senior software engineer produces a technically dense answer that does not waste time on basics. Always tell the AI who the response is for.

Mistake 8: Giving Up After One Try

The first attempt at a prompt is rarely the best one. Iteration is part of the craft. If the output is not what you wanted, examine why. What was missing from the prompt? What was misleading? Refine and try again. Most experienced AI users iterate on a prompt three to five times before they consider it dialed in. Beginners often try once and conclude the AI is not capable, when in reality the prompt is what needed work.

> **The Beginner's Mantra**
>
> If the output is bad, the first place to look is the prompt, not the AI. Most disappointing AI output traces back to a prompt that was too vague, too crowded, or too disconnected from context.

2.6 Chapter Recap and Reflection

This chapter examined the mechanics of how prompts influence output. We covered five major levers and a list of common pitfalls. Let us consolidate the most important ideas before moving on.

- Clarity means a prompt has only one reasonable interpretation. Ambiguity forces the AI to guess.
- Specificity is the right amount of detail for the task. Too little produces generic output. Too much can constrain creativity.
- Context, in five categories, helps the AI position its response correctly. Personal, audience, situational, reference, and stylistic context all play different roles.
- Stating intent and expected outcome explicitly steers the AI toward the right kind of response.
- Eight common beginner mistakes account for most disappointing AI outputs. Recognizing them is the first step to avoiding them.

Reflection Exercise

Work through this audit on three real prompts you have written recently. The numbered steps below give you a repeatable process for evaluating any prompt against this chapter's principles.

1. Select three prompts you have actually used in the past week. Use real examples, not invented ones.
2. Read each prompt against the eight beginner mistakes listed in this chapter.
3. Write down which mistakes, if any, your prompt commits. Be honest. Most prompts commit at least one.
4. Rewrite each prompt to fix the issues you identified.
5. Run both versions and compare the outputs. Note how the rewritten version usually feels longer, more grounded in context, and clearer about the desired outcome.

That gap between the two versions is the gap between an amateur prompt and a professional one. Closing it consistently is the work of the rest of this book.

Bridge to Chapter 3

We have now covered what a prompt is and how prompts influence output. In the next chapter, we will examine the anatomy of a strong prompt in detail, breaking it into its component parts so that you can construct excellent prompts by design rather than by accident.

2.7 The Anatomy of Ambiguity in Detail

In section 2.1 we surveyed the major sources of ambiguity in prompts. Here we go deeper. Ambiguity is worth a careful look because it is the single most common cause of disappointing AI output, and because most ambiguity is invisible to the writer until a careful read reveals it.

Pronoun Trouble

Consider this prompt. Read it and explain how it could fail. The marketing team sent the new logo to the design firm last week, and they liked it. The pronoun they could refer to the marketing team or to the design firm. The pronoun it could refer to the logo, the act of sending, or some implied earlier reference. A human reader might guess the most likely interpretation based on context. The AI also guesses, but its guess may not match yours.

The fix is straightforward. Replace each pronoun with the noun it refers to, even if the result feels slightly redundant. The marketing team sent the new logo to the design firm last week, and the design firm liked the logo. Now the meaning is unambiguous. The output will be aligned with what you actually meant.

Modifier Drift

Modifiers are words that attach to other words to add detail. They cause ambiguity when it is unclear what they attach to. Consider, write a short blog post about productivity for working parents. Does short modify blog post or productivity for working parents? Almost certainly the former, but a strict parse could go either way. Multiplied across a paragraph of prompt, modifier drift can subtly steer the output away from your intent.

The fix is to place modifiers as close as possible to what they modify, and to use punctuation or restructuring when needed. Write a short blog post for working parents about productivity. Now short clearly modifies blog post, and the audience is clearly stated.

Negative Space Ambiguity

Sometimes ambiguity comes from what the prompt does not say. Consider, write a recipe for chocolate chip cookies. The prompt is clear in what it asks for. But it does not specify how many cookies, what kind of chocolate chips, what level of sweetness, what dietary considerations, or what skill level the reader has. The AI will fill these gaps with defaults. The defaults may or may not match what you wanted.

The fix is to anticipate the most consequential gaps and fill them. Write a recipe for two dozen classic chocolate chip cookies, using semi sweet chips, suitable for a beginner home baker. Now the AI does not have to guess at the size, type, or skill level. The output lands closer to what you wanted.

Hidden Assumptions

Every prompt rests on assumptions the writer takes for granted. The danger is that assumptions clear to you may not be clear to the AI. Consider, summarize the article. The article you mean is obvious to you. To the AI, which has not seen anything in particular, the article is whatever you provide in the prompt or, in the absence of provided text, an unspecified reference.

The fix is to surface your assumptions and provide what the AI needs to share them. Summarize the article below in three sentences for a non technical reader. Notice the explicit anchoring to the article below, which forces you to actually include the article in the prompt rather than waving at it.

Conflicting Constraints

Some prompts ask for things that pull in different directions. Be brief but thorough. Be friendly but professional. Be creative but accurate. Each of these instructions is reasonable in isolation, but they impose tension when combined without guidance about which to prioritize.

The fix is to indicate which constraint takes precedence when the constraints conflict. Be friendly but professional, with the priority on professionalism for any sentence that involves money or commitments. Now the AI knows what to do when the two values pull in opposite directions. The output reflects your actual priority structure.

2.8 Specificity Without Over Specification

In section 2.2, we noted that specificity is good but more specificity is not always better. This section explores the practical balance, with examples that show how to recognize over specification and how to back away from it.

The Symptoms of Over Specification

A prompt is over specified when adding more detail no longer improves the output, when the constraints contradict each other, or when the AI's options are reduced to a tiny zone that strips out useful variation. Symptoms include outputs that feel mechanical, identical across attempts despite the task being creative, or oddly shaped because the structural constraints did not fit the content.

The Goldilocks Test

A useful test for specificity is what we will call the Goldilocks test. Run the same task with three versions of the prompt. A loose version with minimal constraints. A tight version with extensive constraints. A medium version that balances. Compare the three outputs. Note which feels most useful, which feels most fitting, which feels most like what you actually wanted. Often the medium version wins, with the loose version being too generic and the tight version being too rigid. The exact ideal varies by task, but the test itself is reliable.

When More Constraints Help

Constraints help most when the task has a clear purpose, when the audience has known expectations, or when the output will be used in a specific downstream context. A blog post for a known audience benefits from constraints on tone, length, and structure. A piece of code for a specific framework benefits from constraints on style, naming, and patterns. A summary destined for a slide deck benefits from constraints on length and bullet structure.

When Constraints Hurt

Constraints hurt most when the task is exploratory, when the goal is to surface ideas you have not thought of yet, or when the value of the output lies in surprise. A brainstorming prompt with too many constraints produces ideas you would have generated yourself. The whole point of brainstorming is to escape your existing patterns, and over constraining cancels that out. A creative prompt with too many constraints produces output that feels designed by committee, satisfying every rule and inspiring no one.

2.9 Context Setting in Practice

Section 2.3 introduced the five categories of context. This section walks through detailed examples of each category in action, showing how the same task changes when different categories of context are added.

The Same Task, Five Times

Consider the simple task, write an introduction for our company website. Below are five versions of the prompt, each adding a different category of context. Notice how each version produces meaningfully different output, even though the underlying task is the same.

Personal Context Added

```
I am the founder of a small accounting firm. I have been writing the website
copy myself and feel my writing is too dry. Write an introduction for our
company website.
```

The personal context tells the AI who is asking and what concerns they bring. The output will tend toward warmer language than a default introduction would, because the writer's stated goal is to add warmth.

Audience Context Added

```
Write an introduction for our company website. Our visitors are mostly small
business owners who are looking for an accountant for the first time and feel
intimidated by the process.
```

The audience context tells the AI who will read the output. The introduction will tend to address the reader's intimidation directly, with reassuring language and an emphasis on accessibility.

Situational Context Added

```
Write an introduction for our company website. We just rebranded from a generic
name to one that emphasizes our focus on small businesses, and the introduction
needs to signal that focus prominently.
```

The situational context tells the AI why the request is being made now. The introduction will tend to highlight the small business focus and signal the new direction the firm is taking.

Reference Context Added

```
Write an introduction for our company website. Use the following bullet points
as the source of facts:  - Founded in 2018 - Based in a mid sized city - Six
person team - Specializes in restaurants and small retail - Average client size
is $500K to $2M revenue
```

The reference context gives the AI material to work from. The introduction will weave these facts into the copy, producing output that is grounded in the firm's actual reality rather than generic placeholders.

Stylistic Context Added

```
Write an introduction for our company website. Match the tone of this example we
like, which comes from a different industry but has the voice we want:  "We are
not the biggest gardening store in town. We are the one that knows your name.
Bring in your sad tomato plant. We will help."
```

The stylistic context teaches the AI the voice you want. The introduction will tend toward short, warm, slightly playful sentences, with a similar rhythm to the example. The example does the work that ten paragraphs of tonal description could not do.

All Five Combined

Now imagine combining all five categories. The personal context, the audience context, the situational context, the reference context, and the stylistic context all in one prompt. The output is no longer a generic company website introduction. It is a tailored, grounded, voice matched introduction for this specific firm at this specific moment, written for this specific audience. This is the power of layered context. Each layer narrows the gap between generic output and what you actually need.

2.10 Twelve More Beginner Mistakes

Section 2.5 covered eight common beginner mistakes. There are more, and they are worth knowing because they account for many of the moments when prompting feels harder than it should.

Mistake 9: Asking the AI to Read Your Mind

Prompts like make this better do not specify which dimension of better. The AI will pick one. Maybe it shortens the text when you wanted it longer. Maybe it adds detail when you wanted it terse. Always specify the axis on which the improvement should happen.

Mistake 10: Using Insider Language Without Defining It

If your prompt uses jargon specific to your field or company, the AI may not interpret it correctly. Phrases like our usual flow, the standard treatment, or the type B approach mean nothing to the AI without definition. Spell out what these mean within the prompt or replace them with descriptions the AI can understand.

Mistake 11: Treating the AI as Adversarial

Some users approach the AI as if it is trying to fail or trick them. They write prompts in confrontational tones, padding them with warnings and threats. This rarely improves output and often distracts the AI from the actual task. Approach the AI as a willing collaborator. Spend your prompt budget on guidance, not warnings.

Mistake 12: Forgetting to Reset

In a long conversation, the context accumulates. The AI brings everything you have said and everything it has produced into each new response. Sometimes this helps. Sometimes it confuses, especially when the conversation has wandered. If output starts feeling stuck or off, start a fresh conversation with a clean prompt. Resetting is often the fastest path to better output.

Mistake 13: Not Reading the Output Carefully

It is easy to skim the AI's response, accept what looks reasonable, and move on. But the difference between the AI's first attempt and a great result is often a small adjustment that you would only notice with a careful read. Read every important AI output as if you were editing it. Notice where it falls short. Iterate from there.

Mistake 14: Trusting Confident Tone as Confidence

AI models are trained to produce confident sounding text. The confidence is a stylistic feature, not a measure of accuracy. A confidently stated wrong answer is still wrong. Always evaluate output on substance, not on tone. Confident wrong answers are particularly dangerous because they invite trust they have not earned.

Mistake 15: Mixing Roles in One Conversation

Sometimes users ask the AI to act as one role, then mid conversation pivot to a different role without clarifying. The AI may carry forward elements of the previous role, producing inconsistent output. When changing roles, do so explicitly, perhaps in a fresh conversation, perhaps with a clear restatement of the new role and what should change.

Mistake 16: Using Prompts as a Substitute for Thinking

AI is at its best when it amplifies your thinking, not when it replaces it. If you do not know what you want, the AI cannot tell you. Vague prompts produce vague output. The most effective AI users do their thinking first, then use prompts to express their thinking precisely. The AI then accelerates the part that follows the thinking, the writing, the formatting, the iteration. The thinking still belongs to you.

Mistake 17: Forgetting That AI Has Limits

AI models are powerful, but they are not omniscient. They cannot access live information unless explicitly equipped with that capability. They cannot read your screen unless you have a tool that provides that. They cannot run your code unless they have a sandbox. Knowing the limits of your specific AI tool is part of using it well. Asking it to do things it cannot do leads to confusion or invented answers.

Mistake 18: Comparing Yourself to Highly Curated Examples

It is easy to look at impressive AI outputs shared online and conclude that your prompts are inadequate. Often, those impressive outputs are the result of dozens of failed attempts curated into one shareable success. Your output will sometimes be uneven, and that is normal. Compare yourself to your own progress, not to selective showcases.

Mistake 19: Skipping Verification on Important Work

AI output looks finished. It is tempting to treat it as ready to publish. But the polish is stylistic, not factual. Verify any specific claim before relying on it for important work. Treat the AI as a brilliant first drafter who occasionally invents details. The verification is your job.

Mistake 20: Not Saving What Works

When a prompt produces excellent output, the temptation is to take the result and move on. But the prompt itself is an asset. Saving it makes future similar tasks faster and more reliable. Build the habit of saving great prompts immediately. Within months your saved library will be one of the most valuable parts of your AI workflow.

2.11 A Closer Look at the Five Output Levers

In section 1.3, we listed five primary levers that shape AI output: topic, format, tone, length, and audience. Here we look at each in finer detail, with examples and decision rules.

Lever 1: Topic

Topic is the subject of the output. It is the broadest lever and the one most beginners specify well. Even casual prompts usually name the topic. The skill is to specify the topic with the right level of focus. Too broad and the output is generic. Too narrow and the output may struggle to reach a useful length.

Compare write about productivity to write about three time management techniques that work for people who hate rigid schedules. The first is broad. The second is focused enough that the AI knows what kind of output makes sense. The skill is calibrating focus to the desired output length. Longer outputs need broader topics. Shorter outputs benefit from narrower ones.

Lever 2: Format

Format is the structural shape of the output. It is the lever most underused by beginners and most powerful when used well. Specifying the format does more than control appearance. It shapes the AI's reasoning by giving it slots to fill.

A useful menu of formats includes paragraph, bulleted list, numbered list, table, question and answer pairs, dialogue, headed sections, JSON object, markdown table, recipe style, and step by step guide. Each is suited to a different kind of content. Match the format to the content, and the AI will produce output that is easier to read and easier to use.

Lever 3: Tone

Tone is the emotional register of the output. It is harder to specify than format because it is qualitative, but it is no less important. The right tone for an output makes the difference between language that lands and language that misses.

Useful tonal descriptors include warm, cool, formal, casual, urgent, calm, playful, serious, optimistic, cautious, direct, gentle, professional, conversational, technical, accessible, encouraging, neutral, energetic, and reflective. Pair two for nuance, like warm but professional or direct but kind. The pairing captures balance that single words cannot.

Lever 4: Length

Length is the quantitative size of the output. Always specify it. The AI's defaults are not yours. Use specific numbers, not vague descriptors. Words, sentences, paragraphs, items, sections, all of these are precise units the AI can hit.

There is a small art to length specification. Specifying maximum length tends to produce output near the maximum. Specifying minimum length tends to produce output near the minimum. Specifying a range tends to produce output near the middle. Specifying exact length tends to produce output that is approximately exact, with some natural variation. Choose the form of length specification that fits how strict you need to be.

Lever 5: Audience

Audience is who the output is for. Of the five levers, audience is the one whose effect on the output is hardest to predict in advance. The AI uses the audience description to set vocabulary, examples, depth, and even structural choices. A prompt that names a five year old audience produces dramatically different output than the same prompt with a senior researcher audience, even when every other lever is identical.

Useful ways to specify audience include role, age, expertise level, time pressure, prior knowledge, motivation, and emotional state. The richer the audience description, the more precisely the AI tunes its output. A vague audience description produces vague tuning. A specific audience description produces specific tuning.

2.12 The Iceberg Principle

Here is a useful concept to close this chapter. We will call it the iceberg principle. Most of the work that goes into a great AI output sits below the surface, in the prompt. The visible response is the tip of the iceberg. The mass of context, constraints, examples, format, and audience awareness underneath is what holds it up.

Beginners often look only at the tip. They see disappointing output and conclude the AI is the problem. Skilled prompt writers know that the iceberg is mostly hidden, and that the way to improve the tip is to enrich what lies beneath. Most output problems are prompt problems. Most prompt problems are surface area problems. Adding the right kinds of context, constraints, and structure expands the iceberg, and the visible output gets better as a result.

> *Prompts are icebergs. The visible request is small. The hidden mass that gives it shape is what does the real work. Build the hidden mass deliberately, and the visible output rises to meet it.*

Bridge to the Next Section

We have laid the foundations. We know what a prompt is, how it influences output, and what to avoid. Now we are ready to build. The next chapters move from understanding to construction, looking at the anatomy of strong prompts, the design patterns that suit different tasks, and the techniques that elevate routine prompting to expert practice.

2.13 Twenty Detailed Comparisons of Vague Versus Specific Prompts

To make the difference between vague and specific prompts visceral, here is a catalog of twenty side by side comparisons. Each pair takes the same general task and shows the vague version next to a specific version. Notice the patterns. Notice how often the specific version is two to three times longer than the vague version, but how dramatically the specificity changes what the AI can produce.

Vague Prompt	Specific Prompt
Make this email shorter.	Cut this email to under 80 words while preserving the apology and the offer of a discount. Maintain a warm, accountable tone.
Help me write a resume.	Update the resume below for a senior product manager role at a B2B SaaS company. Emphasize cross functional leadership and quantifiable outcomes. Use 200 words per role.

Vague Prompt	Specific Prompt
Tell me about climate change.	Explain the difference between climate adaptation and climate mitigation in 200 words for a high school audience. Use one concrete example of each.
Write a story.	Write a 500 word short story about a librarian who finds a key. The tone should be warm and slightly mysterious. End with a question rather than a resolution.
Make a study guide.	Create a one page study guide for the AP Biology unit on cellular respiration. Include three labeled sections: key terms, key processes, and three sample questions with answers.
Summarize this document.	Summarize the document below in 150 words for a busy executive. Lead with the bottom line, then list the three most important findings, then suggest one decision the executive should consider.
Give me marketing ideas.	Generate seven marketing ideas a solo founder of a productivity app could test in the first month after launch with a $300 budget. Format as a numbered list with one sentence pitch and one sentence rationale per idea.
Help me name my product.	Suggest twelve possible names for a subscription service that delivers monthly themed boxes of high quality stationery. Names should be one or two words, evoke craft and quality, and be easy to spell. Avoid names that include the word stationery.
Translate this.	Translate the email below from English to Brazilian Portuguese. Maintain the warm,

Vague Prompt	Specific Prompt
	professional tone of the original. Preserve any product names in their original spelling.
Edit my essay.	Edit the essay below for clarity and flow. Preserve the voice and arguments. Cut any sentences that are repetitive or that do not add new information. Mark each cut with a brief comment so I can decide whether to accept it.
Plan my trip.	Plan a four day itinerary for two adults visiting Lisbon for the first time. Include one major attraction per day, two restaurant recommendations per day, and a single neighborhood walk for the final morning. Avoid tourist traps. We prefer pastry, jazz, and second hand bookshops.
Improve my code.	Refactor the Python function below for readability and error handling. Preserve the function signature and behavior. Add a docstring and inline comments where they would help a junior developer.
Write a thank you note.	Write a 75 word thank you note to my mentor for helping me prepare for a job interview last week. Mention specifically that her advice about asking three thoughtful questions was useful. Tone should be warm and personal, not formal.
Tell me about leadership.	Explain the difference between transactional and transformational leadership styles in 250 words. Use one example of each from a non corporate context (sports, military, education, etc.). End with a single sentence about which style fits a fast growing startup.

Vague Prompt	Specific Prompt
Help me apologize.	Draft an apology to a friend whose birthday I forgot. Acknowledge the lapse, take responsibility without excessive grovelling, and propose a specific way to make it up to her. Tone should be warm and slightly self deprecating. Length: under 100 words.
Make this clearer.	Rewrite the paragraph below to be clearer for a non technical reader. Replace any jargon with plain language. Break long sentences. Preserve the technical accuracy of the claims.
Give me tips.	Give me five practical tips for sleeping better tonight, given that I am traveling across three time zones tomorrow morning. Format as a numbered list with one sentence per tip.
Write copy for our website.	Write a 100 word hero section for our website. Our product is a budgeting app for couples. The audience is partners new to merging finances. Tone should be encouraging and judgment free. Include one specific feature mention and a call to action button text.
Help me understand this.	Explain in 200 words how compound interest works for a fourteen year old. Use one concrete example of a small monthly investment compounding over thirty years. Include the math but explain each step.
Write a speech.	Write a 90 second wedding toast for my younger brother. Mention that we played football together as kids, that he is the more disciplined sibling, and that his fiancee makes him laugh harder than anyone I know. Tone should be warm and slightly funny, not sentimental.

As you read these pairs, notice that the specific versions all share certain elements: clear length specifications, named audiences, specified tones, defined formats, and grounded context. Every specific version is doing the same kinds of work, just adapted to different tasks. This is the underlying pattern. Once you can spot it, you can apply it to any prompt you write.

2.14 Practice Drills for Prompt Specificity

To build the habit of specificity, try these drills. Each takes only a few minutes, but the cumulative effect over weeks is significant.

Drill 1: The Length Drill

For the next ten prompts you write, specify a length. Words, sentences, paragraphs, bullets, sections, any unit will do. Notice how the output changes when you include length specification.

Drill 2: The Audience Drill

For the next ten prompts you write, specify an audience. Notice how different audiences produce different vocabulary, depth, and examples even when the topic stays the same.

Drill 3: The Format Drill

For the next ten prompts you write, specify a format. List, paragraph, table, headed sections. Notice how the format choice shapes both the output and how the AI seems to think through the task.

Drill 4: The Tone Drill

For the next ten prompts you write, specify a tone. Notice how the same content takes on different feelings when the tone shifts.

Drill 5: The Context Drill

For the next ten prompts you write, add at least one sentence of context that the AI would not otherwise have. Notice how the output becomes more grounded in your specific situation.

Drill 6: The Constraint Drill

For the next ten prompts you write, add at least one constraint that excludes something you do not want. Notice how the output becomes more aligned with your actual needs.

These six drills, run for a week each, give you a six week course in prompt specificity. By the end, the habits will feel automatic. You will not have to remember to add length, audience, format, tone, context, and constraints. You will reach for them as naturally as you reach for words when speaking.

2.15 The Disappointment Loop and How to Break It

Many beginners experience what we will call the disappointment loop. They write a prompt. The output disappoints. They conclude the AI is not as smart as advertised. They give up or rely on the AI only for trivial tasks. The disappointment confirms their initial skepticism, and they never develop the skills that would have changed everything.

Breaking the loop requires recognizing that disappointment is a signal, not a verdict. The AI's output reflects what your prompt asked for. If the output is generic, the prompt was probably generic. If the output is wrong, the prompt likely lacked the context to be right. If the output is misshapen, the prompt likely lacked structure.

This reframing is uncomfortable at first because it places the responsibility on the user. But it is also empowering. If your prompts are the lever, then improvement is in your hands. You can develop the skill. You can break the loop. The disappointment becomes a diagnostic rather than a verdict.

The Diagnostic Habit

When an output disappoints, before rewriting, run a quick diagnostic. Ask, what specifically about this output is not what I wanted? Is it the topic, the format, the length, the tone, the depth, the specificity? Once you have named the dimension, the repair is targeted. Most disappointments come from one or two specific issues, not from a general failure of the AI. Naming them is the first step to fixing them.

> **From Disappointment to Diagnosis**
>
> When the output disappoints, the temptation is to give up or to vaguely rewrite. The discipline that separates skilled prompters is to diagnose first. What specifically is off? What dimension drifted? Once named, the fix is targeted, and the output improves on the next try.

2.16 The Subtle Power of Question Versus Instruction

In Chapter 1, we noted that questions and instructions produce different kinds of output. Questions invite informational answers. Instructions invite action. This section examines the subtle power of choosing between them deliberately, and the situations where each is the right move.

When Questions Work Best

Questions are the right form when you genuinely want information rather than action. What are the main causes of inflation? How does insulin regulate blood sugar? Who painted The Night Watch? In these cases, a question gets you what you want without unnecessary structure.

Questions also work when you are exploring a topic and do not yet know what action you want. Question driven exploration is a useful pattern for learning. As you discover what you actually need, you can pivot to instruction driven prompts that produce specific deliverables.

When Instructions Work Best

Instructions are the right form when you want a specific deliverable. Write me an email. Draft a contract. Generate ten ideas. Compose a poem. Each of these is a request for action, not just information. Instructions name what you want produced.

Instructions also work when the answer to a question would be unsatisfying as just a paragraph of prose. If you would prefer a structured output, an instruction with format guidance produces it. If you would prefer a complete deliverable, an instruction with constraints produces it.

The Hybrid

Sometimes a question and an instruction work better together than either alone. What are the main causes of inflation? Then explain each in two sentences and rate how relevant each is to the current US economy in 2026. The question opens the topic. The instruction shapes the output. The hybrid produces structured information that fits a specific purpose.

2.17 Real World Conversations: Annotated Examples

Below are three short transcripts of real prompting conversations, lightly fictionalized but representative. Each is annotated to show what the prompter is doing and why.

Transcript 1: Drafting a Difficult Email

```
[User] I need to email a colleague about a project handoff. The colleague did
not document anything before going on leave, and I am picking up the work cold.
I am frustrated but do not want to seem accusatory.  [Annotation] The user
provided rich context: situation, emotional state, and what to avoid. This sets
the AI up to produce appropriate output.  [AI] Drafts an email that acknowledges
the situation neutrally and asks for help locating any informal notes.  [User]
```

```
Make it warmer at the start. The colleague is generally a good person, and I
want to maintain the relationship.  [Annotation] Targeted iteration based on
what the first draft did not capture: the underlying relationship.  [AI] Revises
with a warmer opening that acknowledges the colleague's general reliability.
[User] Good. Now shorten it to under 100 words.  [Annotation] Final length
adjustment. The user took three iterations to reach a strong final version. Each
iteration was small and targeted.
```

Transcript 2: Building a Marketing Brief

```
[User] Help me think through marketing strategy for our new productivity app.
[Annotation] Initial prompt is exploratory rather than action oriented. The user
is using the AI to help structure their thinking.  [AI] Asks clarifying
questions about target audience, budget, timeline, and existing assets.  [User]
Provides answers in a single paragraph.  [AI] Produces a structured strategy
outline with three phases.  [User] The first phase feels right but the second
phase is not specific enough. Give me three concrete tactics for the second
phase, each tied to the audience we discussed.  [Annotation] The user is
iterating on a specific weakness, not vaguely asking for improvement. They named
what was missing (specificity) and the criterion for the fix (tied to the
audience).  [AI] Provides three tactics with specific tie ins.  [User]
Excellent. Now turn the whole thing into a brief I can share with my team. Two
pages, formatted with headings.
```

Transcript 3: Personal Decision Support

```
[User] I am deciding between two job offers. One is at an established company
with stability and modest growth potential. One is at a startup with higher
upside but more risk.  [Annotation] Personal context provided. The AI knows the
situation but not yet what kind of help is wanted.  [AI] Asks what factors
matter most and what the user is currently leaning toward.  [User] Provides a
list of factors and notes a slight lean toward the startup.  [AI] Produces a
structured analysis weighing each factor.  [User] Now play devil's advocate.
Argue strongly for the established company.  [Annotation] The user is using a
follow up to stress test their lean. This is a sophisticated use of AI for
thinking, not just for output.  [AI] Produces a strong case for the established
company.  [User] One more pass. Walk me through the factors I should weigh in
the next 48 hours before making the decision.  [Annotation] Final practical
synthesis.
```

Each of these transcripts shows iterative, layered prompting. The user is not trying to get the perfect output in one shot. They are using the AI through multiple short prompts, each targeting a specific need. This is what skilled prompting looks like in practice. The skill is not in any single prompt. It is in the rhythm of the whole conversation.

2.18 Closing the Foundations

This chapter closes section one of the book. We have built the foundation. We know what a prompt is, how prompts influence output, what makes them effective, and what mistakes to avoid. From here, we move into construction. Chapters three and four cover the anatomy of strong prompts and the design patterns that suit different tasks. Chapters five through seven cover the core techniques that elevate routine prompting to skilled practice.

Take a moment to notice what has changed for you in these first two chapters. The vocabulary you now have. The mental models. The mistakes you can now spot in your own writing. These are the foundations. They will support everything that follows. Trust the foundation, and the higher floors of the building will rise easily.

> *The foundations of any practice are deceptively simple. They are simple to state and easy to forget. The masters of any craft remember the foundations even when they have moved far beyond them. The foundations are not basics that you graduate from. They are roots that you keep returning to.*

Chapter 3: Anatomy of a Strong Prompt

In the previous two chapters, we built a foundation. We defined what a prompt is, examined how it influences output, and surveyed the most common ways prompts go wrong. Now we shift from understanding to construction. This chapter is about how to build a strong prompt deliberately, piece by piece.

Strong prompts are not random successes. They have a recognizable structure. When you examine the prompts that consistently produce excellent output across many people, many tools, and many tasks, you find the same four building blocks appearing again and again. These four blocks are the anatomy of a strong prompt. Master them, and you can construct effective prompts for almost any situation.

The Four Building Blocks of a Strong Prompt

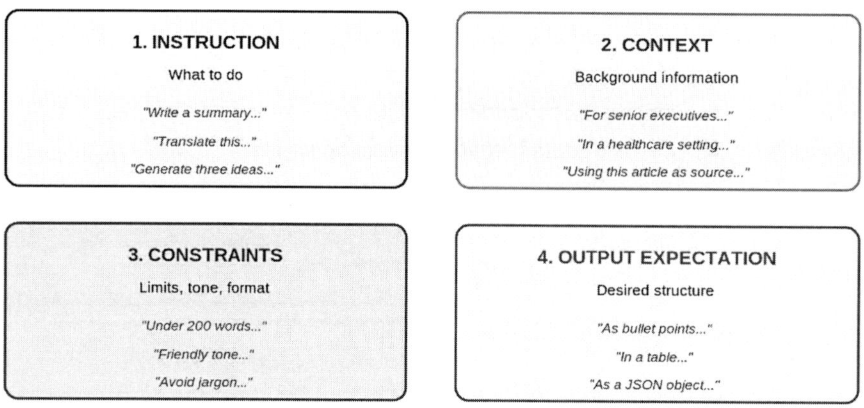

A strong prompt weaves all four together into one coherent message.

Figure 3.1: The four building blocks that compose a strong prompt.

3.1 Instruction: What to Do

The first and most fundamental building block is the instruction. The instruction is the verb of your prompt, the action you want the AI to perform. Without a clear instruction, the AI does not know what kind of work you are asking for. Even a perfectly contextualized prompt is useless without a clear instruction at its heart.

Strong instructions begin with a clear action verb. Write. Summarize. Translate. Compare. Analyze. Explain. Generate. Critique. Outline. Each of these verbs sets a specific expectation about the kind of cognitive work the AI is being asked to perform. They are not interchangeable.

Asking the AI to summarize an article produces a different kind of output than asking it to analyze the same article. Summarize emphasizes compression and faithfulness to the source. Analyze emphasizes interpretation and insight. The verb you choose at the start of your prompt is one of the most consequential decisions you make.

Strong Versus Weak Instructions

A weak instruction is vague, hedged, or disguised as a question. Tell me about marketing. Maybe write something about leadership. Could you possibly help me with this report. These phrasings are polite, but they leave the AI uncertain about whether the user actually wants action and what kind.

A strong instruction is direct and unambiguous. Write a 300 word introduction to email marketing for beginners. Generate five interview questions for a senior product manager candidate. Compare the two software options below across price, features, and ease of use. Each of these starts with a verb and tells the AI exactly what kind of action to take.

Weak Instruction	Strong Instruction	Why the Strong Version Works
Tell me about leadership	Explain three traits of an effective team leader using a real workplace example for each	Specifies action, scope, structure, and a concrete element to include
Help me with this email	Rewrite this email to sound more professional while keeping the message friendly	Action is clear, with two competing constraints balanced
Make this code better	Refactor this Python function to reduce nested loops and add type hints	Names exact improvements rather than asking for vague betterment

Layered Instructions

Sometimes a single verb is not enough. The task requires multiple actions, performed in sequence or in combination. In those cases, you can layer instructions explicitly. First, summarize the article in three sentences. Then, list two questions the article does not answer. Finally, suggest one follow up topic worth exploring. The numbered structure makes the instruction sequence visible to both you and the AI. The output mirrors that structure.

There is a balance to strike here. Layered instructions are powerful but can also create cognitive overload if too many are stacked together. As a rule of thumb, three is comfortable, four is workable, and five or more is usually a sign that the prompt should be broken into a sequence of separate prompts. We will revisit this in Chapter 6 when we discuss step by step prompting in depth.

3.2 Context: Background Information

Context is the second building block. While the instruction tells the AI what to do, context tells the AI what world to do it in. Without context, the AI must rely on its general training data and its statistical sense of what is normal. With context, the AI can position its response specifically for your situation.

In Chapter 2, we introduced five categories of context: personal, audience, situational, reference, and stylistic. In this chapter, we look at how to weave them into a prompt cleanly. The goal is to provide enough context that the AI can do excellent work, without burying the instruction under so much background that the prompt becomes hard to read.

Where to Place Context in a Prompt

There are three common positions for context within a prompt. At the start, context primes the AI before the instruction arrives. In the middle, context refines an instruction with extra details. At the end, context constrains or specifies after the main action has been described. Each position has its uses.

Context at the start works well when the AI's perspective or role needs to be set before the work begins. You might write, you are a marketing strategist with ten years of experience working with consumer brands. Now, write a campaign brief for a new product launch. The role is established first, so the campaign brief that follows comes from that perspective.

Context in the middle works well when the instruction is clear but a specific aspect needs extra detail. You might write, write a 200 word company update. The audience is our remote engineering team, who values direct and technical communication. Focus on the launch metrics from this week. The audience context refines the simple instruction without preceding it.

Context at the end works well as a refinement layer, especially for constraints and stylistic guidance. You might write, write an article about productivity. Use a friendly conversational tone. Include at least one personal anecdote. Avoid corporate jargon. Each of these end constraints sharpens the previous instruction without disrupting its flow.

Avoiding Context Overload

A frequent mistake when learning to prompt well is to over correct from too little context to too much. The result is a wall of background that obscures the actual request. The AI may even weight the wrong details, since when many details compete, the prompt loses focus.

Each piece of context should answer a specific question the AI would otherwise have to guess at. Who are you? Who is the audience? What has happened to make this request necessary? What source material should the AI use? What style or tone is required? If a sentence of context does not address one of those questions, consider whether it belongs in the prompt at all.

> **Context Quality Test**
>
> For every sentence of context in your prompt, ask: would removing this sentence cause the AI to produce different output? If yes, keep it. If no, cut it. Lean prompts with high signal density consistently outperform sprawling prompts with redundant background.

3.3 Constraints: Limits, Tone, and Format

The third building block is constraints. Constraints are the boundaries within which the AI should operate. They define the size, shape, voice, and character of the output. While context tells the AI about the world, constraints tell the AI about the response itself.

Constraints fall into several categories. Length constraints specify how long the output should be. Tonal constraints specify the voice and emotional register. Stylistic constraints specify the writing approach. Content constraints specify what to include or avoid. Format constraints specify the visual structure of the output.

Length Constraints

Length is the simplest constraint to specify and one of the most useful. AI models can produce output of almost any length, but without guidance they default to verbose, explanatory responses. If you want something tight and focused, you must say so. Specify a word count, a sentence count, a paragraph count, or a bullet count. Be explicit. The output will follow your guidance.

Examples of effective length constraints include: in 100 words or fewer, exactly five bullet points, three short paragraphs, two sentences, no more than one paragraph, and a single page summary. Each of these gives the AI a clear target.

Tonal Constraints

Tone is harder to specify because it is qualitative rather than quantitative. But it is no less important. Tone is what makes an output feel right or wrong for its purpose. A formal email and a casual text message can convey the same information yet feel completely different, and the difference is tone.

Common tonal constraints include: warm and conversational, formal and respectful, technical and precise, encouraging but honest, dry and matter of fact, urgent and direct. The more specific your tonal description, the more reliably the AI matches it. Pairing two tonal descriptors is often more useful than one alone, because it captures the nuance better.

Format Constraints

Format constraints specify the visual organization of the output. Bulleted list. Numbered list. Markdown table. JSON object. Three paragraphs. Question and answer pairs. Headed sections. Each of these formats serves a different purpose, and asking for the right one saves a great deal of post processing.

Format constraints are particularly powerful when combined with downstream uses. If you plan to paste the output into a slide deck, request short headlines and bullet points. If you plan to feed the output into a spreadsheet, request a structured table. If you plan to use the output programmatically, request a strict JSON format with named fields.

Content Constraints

Content constraints describe what should or should not appear in the output. Use only the data provided. Do not invent statistics. Avoid clichés. Include at least one example. Use plain language only. These constraints shape the substance of the response, not just its length or look.

Negative content constraints, the do nots, are sometimes necessary but should be used sparingly. As discussed in Chapter 2, positive guidance is almost always more effective than negative guidance. Whenever possible, rephrase a do not as a do. Instead of do not be too technical, write use everyday language a non specialist would understand.

3.4 Output Expectation: Desired Structure

The fourth and final building block is output expectation. While constraints describe the rules of the output, output expectation describes the shape and presentation. The two overlap but are distinct. A constraint might say keep it under 200 words. An output expectation might say structure the response as three labeled sections: Background, Findings, and Recommendations.

Specifying output expectation explicitly is one of the most reliable ways to elevate the quality of an AI response. Without it, the AI must invent its own structure, often producing a competent but generic format. With it, the AI can put its energy into the substance of the response, knowing the structure has already been decided.

Common Output Expectations

Output Expectation	Best Used For	Example Phrasing
Structured paragraphs	Articles, explanations, analyses	Three short paragraphs, each focused on one idea
Bullet list	Quick takeaways, scanning, lists of distinct items	Five bullet points, each starting with an action verb
Numbered list	Steps, rankings, sequences	A numbered list of seven steps in execution order
Table	Comparisons, structured data, side by side analysis	A markdown table with columns: Option, Pros, Cons
Q and A	Educational material, FAQ generation	Five question and answer pairs with bold questions
JSON / structured data	Programmatic use, data extraction	A JSON object with the keys: title, summary, tags

Why Output Expectation Matters So Much

Setting an output expectation does more than control formatting. It actually shapes the AI's reasoning. When the AI knows it must produce a numbered list of seven steps, it organizes its thinking into seven distinct steps. When it knows it must produce a comparison table with three columns, it ensures its analysis covers all three columns for each option. The output structure becomes a mental scaffold the AI builds against.

This is why prompts that specify output expectation often produce more thorough, more balanced, and more useful responses, even on the same underlying task. The structure forces completeness. The shape encourages parallelism. Implicit gaps become visible because the structure has empty slots that demand to be filled.

3.5 Combining All Elements Effectively

The four building blocks are powerful individually. They are transformative when combined. A prompt that includes a clear instruction, well placed context, thoughtful constraints, and a defined output expectation reliably produces excellent output across a wide range of tasks. The combination is what we call a complete prompt.

Building a complete prompt does not have to take much time. With practice, you can compose all four blocks in under a minute for most tasks. The mental discipline matters more than the time spent. Just asking yourself, what is my instruction, what context does the AI need, what constraints apply, and what should the output look like, before you start typing, transforms the quality of your prompts.

A Worked Example

Let us walk through the construction of a complete prompt for a real task. Suppose you need to write a short company update about a recent product launch, intended for the customer support team.

Start with the instruction:

```
Write a company update about our recent product launch.
```

That instruction is clear but generic. Add context:

```
Write a company update about our recent product launch. The audience is our
customer support team, who will use this update to brief themselves before
customer calls. They need to know what changed, why it changed, and what kinds
of customer questions they should expect.
```

Now add constraints:

```
Write a 250 word company update about our recent product launch. The audience is
our customer support team, who will use this update to brief themselves before
customer calls. They need to know what changed, why it changed, and what kinds
of customer questions they should expect. Use a clear and direct tone. Avoid
marketing language. Stick to facts the team can repeat to customers.
```

Finally, add output expectation:

```
Write a 250 word company update about our recent product launch. The audience is
our customer support team, who will use this update to brief themselves before
customer calls. They need to know what changed, why it changed, and what kinds
of customer questions they should expect. Use a clear and direct tone. Avoid
marketing language. Stick to facts the team can repeat to customers. Structure
the response with three short labeled sections: What Changed, Why It Changed,
and Likely Customer Questions.
```

Notice how each layer added a dimension. The instruction was clear from the start. The context oriented the AI to the audience and purpose. The constraints sharpened the tone and forbade marketing language. The output expectation gave the response a structure that reads cleanly and is easy to consume. The final prompt is longer than the original, but it is also vastly more useful.

Diagnosing a Prompt Using the Four Block Model

The four block model is also a powerful diagnostic tool. When a prompt produces disappointing output, you can ask which block is missing or weak. Often the answer is obvious in hindsight. The instruction was vague. The context was missing. The constraints were absent. The output expectation was undefined. Identifying the weak block tells you exactly what to add for the next iteration.

> **Anatomy Checklist**
>
> Before sending any non trivial prompt, check that it contains all four blocks. Instruction: a clear action verb. Context: enough background for the AI to position the response. Constraints: the rules the output must follow. Output expectation: the structure the response should take.

3.6 Chapter Recap

This chapter unpacked the anatomy of a strong prompt. Let us consolidate the key ideas before moving on to design patterns in Chapter 4.

- Strong prompts have four recognizable building blocks: instruction, context, constraints, and output expectation.
- The instruction is the action verb that drives the prompt. Strong instructions are direct and specific.
- Context positions the response for your situation. It can sit at the start, middle, or end of the prompt.
- Constraints define the rules of the output, including length, tone, format, and content.
- Output expectation specifies the structure the response should take, which often improves the underlying quality of the response.
- Combining all four blocks produces what we call a complete prompt. Use the four block model both as a construction guide and as a diagnostic tool.

Practice Exercise

This exercise builds intuition for which of the four building blocks carries the most weight in different situations.

1. Choose three tasks you would normally ask an AI to help with. Pick tasks of different types, for example a writing task, an analysis task, and a planning task.
2. For each task, build a complete prompt that includes all four blocks: instruction, context, constraints, and output expectation.
3. Run each prompt and note the quality of the output.
4. For each task, deliberately remove one block at a time and run the prompt again. Repeat until you have run versions with each of the four blocks individually missing.
5. Compare the outputs across each task. Identify which block, when removed, produced the largest drop in quality.

The block that hurts the most when removed is the one your prompt depends on most heavily for that task. Different tasks lean on different blocks, and noticing this pattern sharpens your judgment for future prompts.

3.7 The Instruction in Depth

Section 3.1 introduced the instruction as the action verb of the prompt. This expanded section examines instruction design more carefully, with attention to the kinds of verbs available, how layering affects output, and how to repair weak instructions efficiently.

A Working Vocabulary of Instruction Verbs

Different verbs invite different kinds of cognitive work from the AI. Building a working vocabulary of instruction verbs gives you precise tools for matching the verb to the task. The list below is not exhaustive, but it covers the verbs you will use most often.

Category	Verbs	When to Use
Generation	write, draft, compose, create, produce, generate	Producing new content from scratch.
Transformation	translate, convert, rewrite, rephrase, transform, reformat	Changing existing content into a new form.
Compression	summarize, condense, distill, abbreviate, abstract	Reducing content while preserving key meaning.
Expansion	elaborate, expand, develop, flesh out, extend	Adding depth or breadth to existing content.

Category	Verbs	When to Use
Analysis	analyze, examine, evaluate, assess, critique, review	Producing structured insight about content.
Comparison	compare, contrast, weigh, juxtapose, differentiate	Producing structured comparisons across options.
Classification	classify, categorize, label, tag, sort, group	Assigning items to predefined categories.
Extraction	extract, identify, list, find, pull out, isolate	Pulling specific information from larger content.
Explanation	explain, clarify, describe, illustrate, interpret	Making concepts accessible or understandable.
Recommendation	recommend, suggest, propose, advise	Producing prescriptive output for a decision.

Notice that within each category, the verbs are not perfectly interchangeable. Summarize and distill both compress, but distill suggests a more aggressive reduction with a focus on the essence. Critique and review both analyze, but critique suggests a more evaluative stance. Choosing the verb that fits the precise shape of the task you want produces output that aligns more naturally with your intent.

Anti Patterns in Instruction Phrasing

Several common phrasing patterns weaken instructions. Knowing them helps you avoid them automatically.

- Phrases that hedge, like maybe write, perhaps create, or could you possibly. Hedging dilutes the action and signals uncertainty about whether you really want it.
- Phrases that frame as questions when you want action, like would it be possible to summarize. The AI may answer the question yes, it would be possible without performing the action.
- Phrases that pile up adverbs, like very carefully and thoroughly write something deeply considered. Adverb stacking does not actually instruct the AI. It is verbal padding.
- Phrases that delay the verb, like in this case, considering all the above factors and given the constraints we are operating under, write. The verb gets buried under qualifiers. Move it to the front.

- Phrases that double instruct, like summarize and explain. The AI must do two things and may compromise on each. Pick one or be explicit about the order.

3.8 Context as a Structured Layer

Section 3.2 covered context placement. This expansion looks at how to structure context as a deliberate layer in your prompts, with patterns for different kinds of source material and different relationships between context and instruction.

Context as a Frame

One useful way to think about context is as a frame around your instruction. The frame establishes who, what, and where. The instruction tells the AI what to do within that frame. When the frame is clear, the instruction can be relatively brief because the frame has already done much of the work. When the frame is unclear, the instruction must carry more weight, often becoming overloaded.

Consider the difference between these two prompts.

```
Write a 200 word response to a customer who is upset that their order arrived
late, explaining what happened and offering a 10 percent discount on their next
purchase, in a tone that is apologetic but not groveling, that fits the voice of
a small artisan bakery rather than a large corporation, and that does not over
promise on future delivery times.
```

```
Frame: You are responding on behalf of a small artisan bakery. The customer's
order arrived late. We want to apologize sincerely without groveling, offer a
small make good (10 percent off next order), and avoid promising what we cannot
guarantee.  Instruction: Write a 200 word response that fits the bakery's warm,
human voice.
```

Both prompts contain the same information, but the second prompt separates the frame from the instruction visually. The AI parses each section more easily, and you can iterate on either the frame or the instruction without disturbing the other. Structuring context as a labeled frame is one of the small habits that makes complex prompts easier to write and easier to maintain.

Context for Source Material

When you provide source material the AI should work from, the way you mark that material matters. The AI distinguishes more cleanly between your instructions and your source material when the material is set off visually, by labels like Source, Input, or Material below, and by clear delimiters. This becomes critical when the source material is long, when it contains language that could be mistaken for instructions, or when you want the AI to refer back to specific parts of it.

```
I will give you a customer review and ask you to do three things with it. The review starts and ends with three dashes.  --- The service was fast but the food was disappointing. I waited five minutes for cold pasta. I will not be back. --- Now do the following: 1. Identify the customer's main complaint. 2. Suggest one immediate action the restaurant could take. 3. Draft a one paragraph apology response.
```

The dashes around the review create a clear visual boundary. The AI knows that the text inside the dashes is the source material, distinct from your instructions. This separation reduces the risk of the AI mistaking the review's language for instructions and producing strange output.

3.9 Constraints in Detail

Section 3.3 introduced constraints across length, tone, format, and content. This expansion looks at constraint design as a discipline, with attention to which constraints to include for which tasks and how to phrase them so the AI follows them reliably.

The Constraint Hierarchy

Not all constraints are equally important for every task. A useful exercise is to imagine your output and ask which qualities, if violated, would make the output unusable. Those qualities deserve top priority constraints. Other qualities may be nice to have but not essential. Spending most of your constraint budget on the top priority qualities, and only a little on the nice to haves, produces prompts that are tight where it matters and flexible where it does not.

For a customer support email, the top priority might be tone (apologetic but not groveling) and length (under 200 words). The format (paragraph) and audience (customer) might be implicit and not need explicit constraints. Spending your constraint budget on tone and length, and skipping format or audience, keeps the prompt focused on what would otherwise go wrong.

Phrasing Constraints for Reliability

How you phrase a constraint affects how reliably the AI follows it. Several patterns are worth knowing.

1. Use must, do, and should explicitly. Phrases like the response must be in 200 words or fewer or the output should always start with a question are clearer than vague preferences.
2. State both positives and the most likely negative. The output should be friendly and warm, not formal or detached. The negation prevents drift toward the default formal voice.

3. Quantify whenever possible. Three to five bullet points is more reliable than several bullet points. 200 words is more reliable than short.
4. Use deterministic structure when reliability matters. Asking for a markdown table with exact columns named Option, Pros, Cons produces more consistent output than asking for a comparison.
5. Restate critical constraints at the end. Constraints near the end of the prompt often weigh slightly more on the immediate next steps of generation. Repeating the most important ones at the end is a small move that improves compliance.

3.10 Output Expectation as a Design Tool

Section 3.4 introduced output expectation. This expansion treats output expectation not just as a way to format output, but as a design tool for shaping the AI's reasoning. The right output expectation can transform a competent response into an excellent one.

Why Structure Drives Reasoning

When the AI generates output into a structured format, it must fill every slot in that structure. A table with five rows and three columns has fifteen cells that must each be filled. Empty cells would feel incomplete, so the AI works to populate each one. This forces the AI to consider all dimensions for all rows, which surfaces gaps in its analysis that freeform prose would let it skip.

This is why specifying a structured output expectation often improves the underlying analysis, not just the presentation. A structured format demands completeness. A freeform format allows partial coverage. For most analytical tasks, completeness is what you want.

Choosing the Right Structure

Different output structures suit different kinds of work. The choice is not arbitrary.

Output Structure	Best For	Example Prompt
Three labeled paragraphs	Articles or essays with clear sections.	Three labeled sections: Background, Findings, Recommendations.
Numbered list	Steps, rankings, sequences.	Seven numbered steps in execution order.
Bullet list	Ideas of similar weight, scanning lists.	Five bullet points, each one sentence.

Output Structure	Best For	Example Prompt
Markdown table	Side by side comparison, structured data.	A markdown table with columns Name, Price, Best For.
Q and A pairs	Educational, FAQ, dialogue.	Five question and answer pairs with bold questions.
JSON object	Programmatic use, data extraction.	A JSON object with keys: title, summary, tags.
Memo format	Internal communications.	Memo format with To, From, Re, then three short body paragraphs.
Pros and cons table	Decision analysis.	Two column table with Pros and Cons, each row one item.
Decision tree	Branching logic, conditional advice.	Plain text outline with If, Then branches.
Time bounded plan	Project planning.	Day by day plan with bullet items under each day.

The Skeleton First Technique

Here is a powerful pattern. Before writing your full prompt, write the skeleton of the output you want. Write the headers, the column names, the section labels, even some of the bullets, with the actual content blank. This skeleton is the output expectation made concrete. Then include the skeleton in your prompt and ask the AI to fill it in.

```
Fill in the skeleton below using the source material I will provide. Do not
change the structure. Match the bullet count and section count exactly.
[Skeleton] What happened: (3 bullets) Why it matters: (2 bullets) What we will
do next: (3 bullets, each starting with an action verb)  [Source material] ...
```

This technique gives you precise control over the shape of the output, much more than describing the structure verbally. The AI follows the skeleton because the skeleton is concrete, not abstract. Use this pattern when you need consistent structured output across many similar tasks.

3.11 Combining the Building Blocks: Three Worked Examples

To make the four building blocks tangible, here are three full worked examples of complete prompts for very different kinds of tasks. Each shows the four blocks in action and explains why each block was included.

Worked Example 1: Customer Outreach Email

```
[Role] You are an experienced customer success manager at a B2B SaaS company.
[Context] The customer is a mid sized company that signed up six months ago.
They have logged in only twice in the last 60 days. We want to re engage them
before they churn.  [Instruction] Draft an outreach email to the customer's
primary contact.  [Constraints] Under 200 words. Warm but professional tone. Do
not push features. Do not be apologetic. Do not assume the customer is
dissatisfied. Acknowledge that we have not been in touch lately and offer help.
[Output expectation] Format as a complete email with a subject line, greeting,
body in two short paragraphs, a single closing question, and a signature line.
```

Notice how each block does its work. The role sets the perspective. The context explains the situation. The instruction names the action. The constraints govern tone, content, and what to avoid. The output expectation specifies the email structure. Together, these produce a prompt that yields a usable email on the first try, with little iteration needed.

Worked Example 2: Code Review

```
[Role] You are a senior Python engineer reviewing code for a small web
application.  [Context] The code below is a function that processes user
uploaded CSV files. It works for valid input but has been observed to crash on
malformed input. The team has limited time to fix it.  [Instruction] Review the
code and identify any defects, edge cases, or readability issues. Suggest
improvements.  [Constraints] Focus on issues that affect correctness or
robustness. Do not suggest stylistic changes that are purely cosmetic. Use
language a junior developer can follow.  [Output expectation] Produce three
labeled sections: Defects (numbered list), Edge cases (numbered list),
Readability (numbered list). Under each item, briefly explain the fix.  [Code]
...
```

This prompt would produce a code review that is structured, focused on what matters, accessible to a junior developer, and consistent across reviews of similar code. The structure of the output, with three labeled lists, ensures the AI considers all three dimensions for every issue, rather than producing a freeform review that might focus on one dimension at the expense of others.

Worked Example 3: Strategic Brainstorm

```
[Role] You are a creative strategist who specializes in marketing for small
craft businesses.  [Context] A small ceramics studio in a college town wants to
attract more customers. They have $500 a month for marketing, no social media
presence, and a six person team. Their work is high quality and reasonably
priced.  [Instruction] Generate marketing strategy ideas they could test in
their first month.  [Constraints] Ideas should fit the budget. Each idea should
be testable in 30 days. Avoid generic advice. Lean toward ideas that play to a
craft business's strengths, like in person experiences and community.  [Output
expectation] Produce a numbered list of seven ideas. For each, provide a one
sentence pitch and a one sentence rationale tied to the studio's specific
situation.
```

This prompt produces practical, situation specific ideas rather than the kind of generic marketing advice that fills internet articles. The role primes the AI to think like a small business strategist. The context grounds the ideas in real constraints. The constraints prevent generic suggestions. The output expectation ensures consistent depth across all seven ideas. The result is a usable list, not a wandering essay.

3.12 Diagnostic Questions for Improving Any Prompt

When a prompt is not producing the output you want, asking the right diagnostic questions reveals which block needs attention. Below is a checklist you can run through any time a prompt feels off.

1. Is the instruction clear? Could a different verb describe what I want better?
2. Is the action specific enough? Have I named the exact thing I want produced?
3. Have I provided enough context for the AI to position the output for my situation?
4. Have I named the audience? Different audiences need different language and depth.
5. Have I specified the tone? Default voice often does not fit the situation.
6. Have I specified the length? AI defaults rarely match what you actually want.
7. Have I specified the format? Format choices affect both presentation and reasoning.
8. Are there constraints the AI might guess wrong about that I should make explicit?
9. Are there things I do not want, that I have not stated and the AI may default to?
10. Could I provide an example or two that would teach the AI what I want better than verbal description?

Running through these ten questions before sending an important prompt takes about a minute. The minute pays back many times over in the quality of the output and the reduction in iteration cycles. Make this checklist a habit, and your prompts will improve consistently.

> **The Habit That Compounds**
>
> The single habit that separates skilled prompt writers from beginners is the discipline of running this kind of mental checklist before sending. Skilled writers do it automatically. Beginners hit send and hope. The difference in output quality is not luck. It is the checklist.

3.13 An Extended Catalog of Worked Examples

To deepen the understanding of how the four building blocks work together, here are ten more worked examples spanning different industries and tasks. Read them carefully. Notice the patterns that repeat across them, even though the tasks are very different.

Worked Example 4: Restaurant Concept Pitch

```
[Role] You are a restaurant industry consultant who advises first time
restaurant owners.  [Context] My partner and I are planning to open a small
Mediterranean inspired restaurant in a mid sized college town. We have $200,000
in starting capital and three years of relevant cooking experience but no
business background. The town has plenty of pizza and burger options but limited
Mediterranean choices.  [Instruction] Produce a one page concept summary we can
show potential investors.  [Constraints] Length: under 500 words. Tone:
confident but realistic, not over promising. Avoid generic restaurant industry
cliches. Lean on the specific opportunity in our town.  [Output expectation]
Format as a memo with these sections: Concept Overview, Target Customer,
Differentiation, Financial Outline, and Why Us.
```

Worked Example 5: Customer Research Synthesis

```
[Role] You are a user researcher with experience synthesizing qualitative
interview data.  [Context] We interviewed twelve customers of our subscription
meal kit service. The interview transcripts are below. We want to surface the
most important themes for the product team.  [Source] [Twelve interview
transcripts pasted here]  [Instruction] Identify the four most prominent themes
across the interviews and provide evidence for each.  [Constraints] Use only
quotes and observations from the transcripts. Do not invent themes that lack
evidence. Distinguish between recurring complaints and one off concerns.
[Output expectation] For each theme, produce a labeled section with: Theme name
(one line), Description (one paragraph), Three example quotes from the
transcripts, and Suggested next research questions.
```

Worked Example 6: Performance Review

```
[Role] You are an experienced manager writing performance reviews for direct reports.  [Context] I need to write a six month review for a product designer on my team. They are strong technically but have been less effective on cross functional collaboration this period. I want the review to be honest, supportive, and actionable.  [Instruction] Draft the review.  [Constraints] Tone: warm but candid. Length: under 400 words. Include both strengths and growth areas. Provide specific, observable behaviors rather than abstract assessments. Frame growth areas as actionable rather than as failures.  [Output expectation] Format with three labeled sections: Strengths Demonstrated, Growth Areas, and Goals for Next Period. Each section should have two to three substantive points.
```

Worked Example 7: Technical Documentation

```
[Role] You are a technical writer specializing in developer documentation. [Context] We are documenting a new API endpoint that lets developers retrieve user analytics. The endpoint signature is GET /api/v1/users/:id/analytics. It returns a JSON object with daily active users, session length, and feature usage breakdown for the past 30 days.  [Instruction] Write the API reference documentation for this endpoint.  [Constraints] Audience: junior to mid level developers. Tone: precise and helpful. Include code examples in JavaScript and Python.  [Output expectation] Produce sections: Description (one paragraph), Authentication, Request Parameters, Response Schema, Error Codes, and Code Examples (one for each language).
```

Worked Example 8: Conference Talk Outline

```
[Role] You are a speaker coach who helps technical professionals craft compelling conference talks.  [Context] I am giving a 30 minute talk at a regional engineering conference about our team's experience migrating from monolith to microservices. The audience is mostly senior engineers who have heard a lot of microservices talks already. I want this talk to feel fresh. [Instruction] Produce a talk outline.  [Constraints] The talk should have a clear narrative arc, not just a list of takeaways. Avoid the most common cliches of microservices talks. Lean into the specific surprises we encountered, both good and bad.  [Output expectation] Produce: Title (one option), Talk thesis (one sentence), Outline (six to eight sections with brief descriptions and approximate time per section), and Closing thought.
```

Worked Example 9: Curriculum Design

```
[Role] You are an instructional designer with experience in adult professional education.  [Context] I am developing a one day workshop for managers on giving
```

difficult feedback. The audience is mid level managers with three to seven years of management experience. They have all received feedback training before, so the workshop must offer something fresh. [Instruction] Design the workshop curriculum. [Constraints] Total duration: six hours including breaks. Mix of instruction, practice, and discussion. Avoid generic feedback frameworks they have already heard. Focus on the genuinely hard cases that managers struggle with most. [Output expectation] Produce: Workshop title, Learning objectives (three to four), Schedule (six hours, broken into segments with topic, duration, format, and brief description), and Required materials.

Worked Example 10: Investment Memo

[Role] You are a venture capital associate writing investment memos for the partnership. [Context] We are evaluating a Series A investment in a B2B SaaS company that helps mid sized accounting firms automate their tax preparation workflow. The founders are former Big Four senior managers. The company has 40 customers, $2M ARR, 15% month over month growth, and is raising $8M at a $32M pre money valuation. [Source] [Pitch deck content pasted here] [Instruction] Produce an investment memo. [Constraints] Length: under 800 words. Tone: analytical, balanced, surfacing both the case for and against the investment. [Output expectation] Produce sections: Company Snapshot, Market and Opportunity, Team Assessment, Risks, Comparable Outcomes, and Recommendation with one paragraph rationale.

Worked Example 11: Crisis Communication

[Role] You are a crisis communications advisor for a small business. [Context] We just discovered that one of our team members has been making public social media posts that contradict our company values. Customers have started noticing and tagging us. We need a public statement within 24 hours. [Instruction] Draft the public statement. [Constraints] Length: under 200 words. Tone: serious and accountable, not defensive. Acknowledge the issue clearly. State concrete actions. Avoid hedging language and corporate non apologies. [Output expectation] Format as a single block of text suitable for posting on our blog and linking from social media. Include a clear opening that acknowledges the situation, a middle that names what we are doing, and a close that invites further dialogue.

Worked Example 12: Donation Appeal

[Role] You are a fundraising copywriter for small nonprofits. [Context] A local literacy organization needs to raise $50,000 by year end to maintain their after school tutoring program. They have a list of 1,200 past donors. Average past

```
gift is $75. The organization has been operating for 12 years and has tutored
over 800 children.  [Instruction] Draft a donation appeal email.  [Constraints]
Length: under 250 words. Tone: warm and urgent without being manipulative.
Include one specific child story (you can compose a fictional but realistic
example). End with a clear ask and a button text.  [Output expectation] Format
as a complete email with subject line, body in three paragraphs, and call to
action.
```

Worked Example 13: Product Launch Strategy

```
[Role] You are a product launch strategist with experience in mid market
software.  [Context] We are launching version 2 of our project management tool
in eight weeks. The new version has a substantially different user interface,
several new features, and addresses three top complaints from our current
customer base. We have 2,000 active customers and need them to migrate while
also using the launch to attract new customers.  [Instruction] Produce a launch
plan.  [Constraints] The plan should cover the eight weeks before launch and the
four weeks after. It should balance attention to existing customers (avoid
alienation) with attention to new customer acquisition.  [Output expectation]
Produce: Launch overview (one paragraph), Week by week timeline (twelve weeks
total, with two to four key activities per week), Risk callouts (three to five),
and Key metrics to track.
```

Notice the patterns across all of these examples. Every prompt has a clear role, a specific context, a single instruction, well chosen constraints, and a defined output expectation. Every prompt is two to three paragraphs of careful setup, not a one liner. The investment in setup pays back many times over in the quality of what comes out. This is the working pattern of skilled prompting.

3.14 The Elements That Separate Good From Great Prompts

Beyond the four building blocks, there is a more subtle layer of craft that separates good prompts from great ones. These elements are not always strictly necessary, but they consistently elevate quality.

Element 1: A Specific Source of Truth

Great prompts often anchor the AI to a specific source: a document, a transcript, a set of facts, an example. The AI works from this source rather than from its general training. The output is grounded, accurate, and aligned with reality. Without a source of truth, the AI must invent. Inventions are sometimes lovely and sometimes wrong.

Element 2: An Audience With a Pulse

Great prompts describe the audience as a real person with motivations, concerns, and time pressures. Not just a senior executive but a senior executive who has been in five back to back meetings and will read this in two minutes. This level of specificity changes the output dramatically. Generic audience descriptions produce generic output.

Element 3: A Constraint That Shows Restraint

Great prompts often include a constraint that prevents over reach. Avoid generic platitudes. Do not include caveats. Skip the corporate language. These prohibitions remove the kinds of weak content that AI defaults to. The remaining content is concentrated value.

Element 4: A Standard for Quality

Great prompts sometimes name what good output looks like. The output should be clear enough that a senior executive could grasp it in 90 seconds. The story should land emotionally on the first read. The recommendation should be actionable today, not theoretical. These standards orient the AI toward a specific kind of excellence.

Element 5: A Touch of Personality

Great prompts sometimes include a small note about voice or sensibility. Slightly self deprecating. Quietly confident. Warm but not gushing. These touches make output feel like it came from a specific person rather than a generic source. They are small, but they accumulate into significant differentiation.

> **Good Versus Great**
>
> Good prompts include the four building blocks. Great prompts also include source of truth, audience with a pulse, restraint constraints, quality standards, and a touch of personality. The difference between good and great is often these layers of craft, not radical departures.

3.15 The Maintenance of a Strong Prompt

Strong prompts are not built once and used forever. They are maintained over time, just like any working asset. Maintenance includes noticing when output quality drifts, refining when patterns shift, and retiring prompts that no longer serve. Below are practices that keep your strong prompts strong.

Periodic Review

Once a quarter, run your most used prompts and read the output critically. Has it drifted? Are there subtle issues that have crept in? Sometimes models update, sometimes your needs change, and sometimes the prompt that was excellent six months ago is now merely adequate. The periodic review catches drift before it becomes habit.

Targeted Refinement

When you notice drift, refine the prompt rather than rewriting from scratch. Targeted refinement preserves what works while addressing what does not. The discipline of small targeted changes, rather than wholesale rewrites, builds prompts that improve incrementally over years.

Version History

Keep version history of your most important prompts. When you refine, save the previous version. Sometimes a refinement that seems like an improvement turns out to produce worse output for some inputs. Having the previous version lets you roll back.

Documentation Updates

When you refine a prompt, update its documentation. Note what changed and why. Future you will appreciate knowing the reasoning behind the current version. Without documentation, you may forget why a prompt has its specific shape and unintentionally undo a thoughtful design choice.

Retirement

Some prompts outlive their usefulness. The task they served no longer applies. Better techniques have replaced them. The audience has changed. Recognize when a prompt has reached the end of its life and retire it. Retired prompts can be moved to an archive rather than deleted, in case the task returns. But removing them from your active library keeps the library focused on what is currently useful.

Chapter 4: Prompt Design Patterns

In Chapter 3, we examined the building blocks of a strong prompt. In this chapter, we look at how those building blocks combine into recurring shapes. Across countless prompts, certain patterns appear again and again, each suited to a specific kind of task. We call these patterns prompt design patterns, and learning them gives you a vocabulary of ready made structures you can adapt and reuse.

Think of design patterns the way an architect thinks of building forms. A bungalow, a townhouse, a high rise, a farmhouse, each has a different shape, suited to a different need. None is inherently better. Each is right for some situations and wrong for others. The skill of an architect lies partly in knowing the patterns and partly in knowing which pattern fits the moment. The same is true for prompt design.

Five Core Prompt Design Patterns

1. Direct Prompt
"What is the boiling point of water at sea level?"
Use for simple, factual, single-step questions.

2. Instruction-Based Prompt
"Convert this paragraph into three concise bullet points highlighting key actions."
Use when you need a transformation or action performed on input.

3. Role-Based Prompt
"Act as a senior copy editor reviewing a magazine article. Critique tone, clarity, and pace."
Use to set perspective, expertise, and standards for the response.

4. Format-Driven Prompt
"Compare these three plans in a markdown table with columns: Name, Price, Best For."
Use when the structure of the output is critical.

5. Multi-Step Prompt
"First analyze the data. Then identify trends. Finally, recommend three actions."
Use for complex tasks that benefit from sequential reasoning.

Figure 4.1: Five core prompt design patterns and the situations they suit best.

4.1 Direct Prompts: Simple Tasks

The direct prompt is the simplest pattern. It consists of a single, clear instruction, often phrased as a short question or command. There is little context, few constraints, and no elaborate output expectation. The direct prompt works because the task itself is simple, common, and well defined.

Examples of direct prompts include: what is the boiling point of water at sea level, give me a one line summary of photosynthesis, what does API stand for, how many time zones are there in Russia. Each of these is a single self contained question that the AI can answer with little ambiguity.

When to Use Direct Prompts

Direct prompts work best when three conditions are true. First, the answer to your question has a relatively narrow correct range. Asking what is the capital of France has essentially one correct answer. Second, the topic is common enough that the AI's training data covers it well. Asking about the history of common everyday concepts is safe. Asking about niche or recent topics may need more guidance. Third, you do not care much about the format of the answer. A factual lookup does not need styling. A short, direct response is exactly what you want.

Limitations of Direct Prompts

Direct prompts struggle with three kinds of tasks. Tasks that require nuance, where the right answer depends on context. Tasks that have many valid forms of output, where the AI must choose between them. And tasks that demand a particular style or audience, since direct prompts give the AI no guidance on either.

If you find yourself dissatisfied with the output of a direct prompt, the answer is usually not to make the question shorter or sharper. It is to upgrade to a richer pattern that includes more of the building blocks. Direct prompts are perfect for what they are designed for. They are the wrong tool for everything else.

> **Direct Prompt Quick Test**
>
> Ask yourself, would I expect a librarian to give me a one or two sentence answer to this question without follow up? If yes, a direct prompt is appropriate. If no, you probably need a richer pattern.

4.2 Instruction Based Prompts

The instruction based prompt is one step up from the direct prompt. It uses a clear action verb, gives the AI input material to work with, and asks for a specific transformation or product. Unlike a direct prompt, which usually asks for a known answer, an instruction based prompt asks the AI to do work.

Examples include: rewrite this paragraph in plain English, translate this email to French, generate three headline options for this article, summarize the key arguments of this essay in three bullet points. Each of these has a clear verb, a clear input, and a clear product.

Anatomy of an Instruction Based Prompt

An instruction based prompt typically follows a recognizable shape. It starts with a verb. It identifies the input. It specifies, if needed, a constraint or format. The shape is, verb, the thing, with these qualities. For example, summarize the article below, in three sentences, focusing on the main argument. The first phrase is the verb. The second phrase identifies the input. The third phrase adds the qualifier.

This shape is intuitive because it mirrors the way humans give instructions to each other in the real world. Bring me the report, the latest one, before the meeting starts. Summarize the meeting notes, in one paragraph, for the people who missed the call. Send the deck, the cleaned up version, to the client by tomorrow. Each of these everyday instructions follows the same verb, thing, qualifier structure.

When Instruction Based Prompts Shine

Instruction based prompts are ideal for clear, transformational tasks. You have something. You want something else. The AI bridges the gap. Editing, translating, summarizing, formatting, expanding, condensing, classifying, all of these are well served by instruction based prompts. The AI is being asked to perform a defined operation on a defined input. There is little room for confusion.

4.3 Role Based Prompts: Act As...

Role based prompts are among the most powerful patterns in modern prompting. The structure is simple. You ask the AI to take on a role, and then you give it a task. By assigning a role, you set the AI's perspective, expertise level, vocabulary, and standards before any specific instruction is processed.

Examples include: act as a senior copy editor reviewing a magazine article, act as a tax accountant explaining quarterly estimated payments to a freelancer, act as a hostage negotiator advising me on a difficult conversation with my landlord, act as a children's book author writing about the solar system. Each of these roles changes the entire flavor of the response, even when the underlying task is similar.

How Roles Shape Output

A role does at least three things to a prompt. First, it sets the perspective the AI should take. A senior copy editor and a junior writer would notice different things in the same article. Second, it sets the vocabulary and tone. A hostage negotiator and a customer service representative speak differently, even on the same topic. Third, it sets the standards. A senior engineer reviewing code expects different qualities than a beginner writing it for the first time.

These three effects compound. Together, they push the AI's output toward a particular zone of the possibility space, narrowing what would otherwise be a vast range of acceptable answers down to a much smaller, more useful range.

Designing Effective Roles

Not all roles are equally effective. The most useful roles share three qualities. They are specific. They are real. And they have visible standards.

Specific roles outperform generic ones. Act as a senior product manager at a B2B SaaS company is more useful than act as a product person. The added specificity tells the AI what kind of work, what kind of audience, and what kind of standards to bring to the response. Real roles, ones that exist in the actual world, outperform invented or whimsical roles. Visible standards mean the role suggests how the work would be evaluated, like an editor evaluating clarity, a doctor evaluating safety, or a teacher evaluating clarity.

Generic Role	Stronger Specific Role	Why It Works Better
A writer	A magazine feature writer for a popular science publication	Sets format, audience, and editorial standards
A teacher	A high school physics teacher creating notes for a sophomore class	Sets level, subject, and audience expectations
A coach	An executive coach helping a new manager prepare for a difficult performance review	Sets context, stakes, and tone
A consultant	A management consultant advising a mid sized retail company on cost reduction	Sets industry, company size, and objective

4.4 Format Driven Prompts: Tables, Lists, and Summaries

Format driven prompts make the structure of the output the central feature of the prompt. Rather than asking the AI to generate freeform prose, you ask it to fit its response into a predefined shape. The format becomes both a constraint on the AI and a delivery vehicle for you.

Examples include: compare these three options in a markdown table with columns Name, Price, and Best For; list the top five risks of this strategy as bullets, each starting with a verb; summarize the meeting notes as five question answer pairs; convert this transcript into a structured action item list with owner and due date columns. In each case, the format does work that prose alone could not do as efficiently.

Why Format Matters More Than It Seems

Format is often treated as cosmetic, but it is anything but. The right format makes information legible at a glance, comparable across items, scannable for the busy reader, and reusable in downstream tools. The wrong format makes the same information feel dense, hard to navigate, and frustrating to repurpose.

A second benefit of format driven prompts is that they often improve the underlying reasoning. When the AI must produce a comparison table with five rows and three columns, it has to consider all fifteen cells. Gaps become visible because the structure demands they be filled. Compare this to a freeform comparison paragraph, where the AI can subtly skip over weak points or imbalanced coverage.

Choosing the Right Format

The right format depends on what the reader needs to do with the output. For at a glance comparison, tables work best. For sequential steps or rankings, numbered lists. For unordered ideas or items of similar weight, bullet lists. For programmatic use, JSON or another structured data format. For Q and A reference material, question answer pairs. For narrative prose, paragraphs. Match the format to the use case, and the format will work for you, not against you.

4.5 Multi Step Prompts

Multi step prompts are the most complex of the core patterns. They string together several actions or stages within a single prompt, often with explicit numbering or labeling. The AI processes each step in order and produces output that reflects the structured progression.

An example multi step prompt might read: First, read the customer feedback below and identify the top three themes. Second, for each theme, suggest one product change that would address it. Third, for each suggested change, estimate whether it is small, medium, or large in engineering effort. Finally, present your output as a markdown table with columns Theme, Suggestion, and Effort.

When Multi Step Prompts Are Worth Their Complexity

Multi step prompts shine when a task has clear sub stages and the value of doing each stage well outweighs the simplicity of asking once. They are particularly useful when the output of an earlier stage informs the output of a later stage, like the way the suggested changes in step two depend on the themes identified in step one. They are also useful when you want to make the AI's reasoning process visible, since each step produces output you can review.

Multi step prompts have limits. If the task has too many stages, the AI may begin to lose coherence between steps, or it may rush through later stages because earlier stages consumed too much attention. As a general guideline, three to five stages per prompt is comfortable. Beyond that, breaking the prompt into a sequence of separate prompts often produces better results. Chapter 6 covers this in depth.

Numbering and Labeling Steps

Multi step prompts work better when the steps are labeled clearly. Use words like first, then, next, finally. Or use numbered structure like 1, 2, 3. Or use named labels like Step One, Step Two. Any of these helps the AI track which stage it is in. Without clear labeling, multi step prompts can blur together, and the output may collapse the stages into a single response that loses the structure you wanted.

4.6 Combining Patterns

The five patterns introduced in this chapter are not mutually exclusive. In practice, sophisticated prompts often combine several patterns at once. A role based prompt might also be format driven, like act as a senior product manager and produce a quarterly review of these features in a markdown table with columns Feature, Status, and Risk. A multi step prompt might also be instruction based at each step. The patterns layer naturally.

As you grow more comfortable with each pattern individually, you will start to combine them without thinking about it. You will reach for a role at the start of a prompt because the task benefits from a perspective. You will specify a format at the end because you know how you want the output to look. You will break the prompt into steps because the task has clear stages. Each pattern earns its place in the prompt, and the result is a structure tailored to the situation.

Pattern Library Mindset

Treat the design patterns as a personal library you draw from. The more patterns you know well, the more flexibly you can respond to any new task. The fewer patterns you know, the more often your prompts will feel forced or off shape.

4.7 Chapter Recap

This chapter introduced five core prompt design patterns and discussed how they fit different kinds of tasks.

- Direct prompts are short, single question prompts suited to factual lookups and well known topics.
- Instruction based prompts use a verb plus an input to perform a specific transformation.
- Role based prompts assign the AI a perspective, which sets vocabulary, standards, and tone.
- Format driven prompts make the structure of the output the focal point and often improve underlying reasoning.
- Multi step prompts string several actions together with clear labeling and work well for tasks with natural stages.
- Patterns combine. The more you know, the more flexibly you can match a structure to the moment.

Practice Exercise

This exercise rapidly builds your intuition for which pattern fits which kind of work.

1. Pick a single task you have been thinking about. It could be writing a brief, analyzing a document, or planning a project.
2. Write a direct prompt version of the task in one short sentence.
3. Write an instruction based version that names a specific action and a clear input.
4. Write a role based version that begins by assigning the AI a relevant role or persona.
5. Write a format driven version that specifies the structure of the output explicitly, such as a table or labeled sections.
6. Write a multi step version that breaks the task into a sequence of clearly labeled stages.
7. Run all five versions and compare the outputs side by side. Notice how the same underlying task produces meaningfully different work depending on which pattern you use.

By the end, you will have a clear personal sense of which patterns suit your most common tasks. That instinct, refined across dozens of prompts, becomes the difference between picking patterns at random and choosing them with intent.

4.8 The Direct Prompt in Practice

Section 4.1 introduced the direct prompt. This expansion looks at common variations and the small adjustments that make even simple direct prompts work better.

Adding a Word of Context to Direct Prompts

Even direct prompts benefit from a small amount of context that disambiguates the question. The capital of France is unambiguous. The latest version of Python may not be, depending on what counts as latest. Adding a word like stable, current, or supported can sharpen the answer significantly.

Compare these direct prompts.

```
How does inflation affect investments?

How does inflation affect long term retirement investments for an individual
investor?
```

Both are direct, but the second produces a more focused, more useful answer because the context narrows the question. The investment of three or four extra words produces output that is much more relevant to a specific situation.

Direct Prompts in Sequence

A surprisingly powerful pattern is to use direct prompts in sequence, where each builds on the last. Each prompt is itself simple, but the conversation as a whole accomplishes complex work. This works because the AI maintains conversational context, so each direct prompt can refer implicitly to what came before.

```
What is photosynthesis? What are the two main types? Give me an example of each.
Which type is more efficient in hot, dry climates?
```

Each prompt is direct. None could stand alone usefully. But in sequence they produce a structured exploration of a topic, with each step refining or extending the previous. This is a useful technique when you want to learn about a topic but do not yet know what specific questions to ask.

4.9 Instruction Based Prompts: Variations and Anti Patterns

Instruction based prompts are workhorses, used for the majority of everyday AI tasks. This expansion covers variations that handle different shapes of input, and anti patterns that weaken instruction based prompts.

Variation 1: Single Input, Single Action

The simplest form is one input plus one action. Translate this paragraph to French. Summarize this article in three bullets. Rewrite this email in a more formal tone. The single input plus single action structure is reliable, predictable, and well suited to small tasks.

Variation 2: Single Input, Multiple Actions

Sometimes you want several things done with one piece of input. Read this article and tell me the three main arguments, then suggest three counter arguments, then identify which side has the stronger case. The pattern is one input plus multiple sequential actions, with the order signaling priority.

Variation 3: Multiple Inputs, Single Action

When you have multiple inputs, the structure changes. Compare these three product descriptions and suggest which is most likely to convert. The action is a single comparison, but the inputs are multiple. Mark the inputs clearly and label them so the AI can refer to them in its analysis.

Variation 4: Multiple Inputs, Multiple Actions

The most complex form combines multiple inputs and multiple actions. For each of these five customer reviews, identify the main concern, suggest a response, and rate the urgency on a scale of one to five. This structure is best supported by a clear output format, like a markdown table, that gives the AI slots to fill consistently across all inputs.

Anti Patterns to Avoid

- Burying the action under qualifiers, like with respect to all the considerations above, please now translate. Move the action to the front.
- Switching subjects mid prompt, like rewrite this paragraph and also tell me about a related topic. The two requests dilute each other.
- Asking for multiple incompatible outputs in one prompt, like provide both a brief summary and a comprehensive analysis. Choose one or sequence them.
- Providing input as if the AI has already seen it, like as I mentioned earlier or based on the document. Always include the input you want the AI to work from.

4.10 Role Based Prompts: A Library of Useful Personas

Section 4.3 introduced role based prompting. This expansion offers a library of useful personas tuned for common tasks, with notes on when each is most effective.

Editorial and Writing Personas

- Senior copy editor for a glossy magazine. Use for editing prose for tone, rhythm, and clarity.
- Plain language coach. Use for translating jargon heavy text into accessible language.
- Headline writer for a tabloid newspaper. Use for punchy, attention grabbing short headlines.
- Memoir writing coach. Use for personal essays and reflective writing.
- Technical documentation specialist. Use for clear, structured documentation of complex systems.

Strategy and Advisory Personas

- Management consultant for mid sized service businesses. Use for cost reduction, growth analysis, organizational design.
- Product strategist for early stage SaaS companies. Use for prioritization, positioning, customer development.
- Marketing strategist for craft and small businesses. Use for low budget creative marketing ideas.
- Career coach for mid career professionals. Use for transition planning, skill development, narrative.
- Communications advisor for crisis situations. Use for difficult announcements, sensitive messaging.

Technical Personas

- Senior Python engineer focused on web applications. Use for code review and architectural advice.
- Database administrator with experience in PostgreSQL. Use for query optimization and schema design.
- Security engineer with a focus on web vulnerabilities. Use for threat modeling and defensive coding.
- DevOps engineer specializing in cloud infrastructure. Use for deployment, monitoring, infrastructure as code.
- Frontend designer who codes. Use for UI components, accessibility, design systems.

Educational Personas

- High school teacher creating notes for a curious student. Use for explaining concepts at a beginner level.
- Graduate level professor explaining a topic to colleagues. Use for advanced explanations with rigor.
- Tutor specializing in math anxiety. Use for gentle, encouraging explanations that build confidence.
- Children's book author writing for ages eight to ten. Use for explanations that use vivid metaphors and accessible vocabulary.
- Trivia host preparing questions for a quiz night. Use for engaging educational content with a competitive edge.

Creative Personas

- Short story writer in the literary realism tradition. Use for grounded fiction with strong character voice.
- Comedy writer for a sitcom about a workplace. Use for funny, character driven dialogue.
- Poet who writes for occasional events like weddings and birthdays. Use for warm, accessible verse.
- Songwriter in the folk tradition. Use for lyrics that emphasize storytelling over wordplay.
- Visual artist describing intended mood and palette. Use for art direction prompts.

> **Building Your Persona Library**
>
> As you encounter tasks that benefit from specific expertise, save the personas that work for you. Over time you will build a library you can reach for instantly. Each persona is itself a small prompt asset.

4.11 Format Driven Prompts: Choosing the Right Format

Section 4.4 covered format driven prompts. This expansion provides a decision guide for choosing among the most useful formats, with examples of each format in action and notes on what they do well and poorly.

Tables

Tables are the right format when you have multiple items to compare across multiple dimensions. The strength of a table is parallel coverage, every item gets the same dimensions, every dimension gets the same items. The weakness is that complex content does not fit well in cells, so tables work best when each cell can be a short phrase rather than a paragraph.

Use tables for: comparisons across options, structured catalogs, before and after, pros and cons, criteria evaluations, and any task where reading across rows or down columns reveals useful patterns.

Numbered Lists

Numbered lists are the right format when order matters. Steps in a process. Items ranked by priority. Stages of a sequence. The numbers carry information, signaling that item three comes after item two and before item four. If order does not matter, use bullets instead, since numbers imply sequence.

Use numbered lists for: instructions, rankings, sequential plans, step by step procedures, and any task where the position of an item conveys meaning.

Bulleted Lists

Bulleted lists are the right format when items are distinct but unordered. Reasons in support of a position. Features of a product. Risks to consider. Bullets signal that the items are siblings, not a sequence. Each bullet should be self contained and roughly parallel in scope.

Use bulleted lists for: scanning, ideation, feature lists, considerations to weigh, and any task where the reader will not necessarily read every item in order.

Headed Sections

Headed sections are the right format when content is long enough that the reader needs navigation. A headed section is essentially a label plus a paragraph or two of prose. The labels guide the reader to the part they care about. They also force the writer to organize content into distinct themes rather than letting it run together.

Use headed sections for: reports, articles, briefings, deliverables longer than a few hundred words, and any output the reader will scan rather than read straight through.

JSON or Structured Data

Structured data formats are the right choice when the output will feed into other software. JSON, YAML, CSV, and similar formats let you specify exactly the keys and values you want. The AI fills the structure precisely, producing output that other tools can consume without parsing.

Use structured data for: data extraction, programmatic pipelines, integrations with other tools, and any task where downstream automation matters.

Question and Answer

Question and answer pairs are the right format for FAQ documents, educational material, and any task where the reader's likely questions are the natural unit of organization. Each question becomes a section, with the answer underneath. The format makes it easy to add and remove items without restructuring.

Use Q and A for: FAQ pages, study guides, common objection handling, interview prep, and any educational content organized around questions a learner would actually ask.

4.12 Multi Step Prompts: Patterns and Limits

Section 4.5 introduced multi step prompts. This expansion examines several useful patterns and discusses where multi step prompts begin to lose their effectiveness.

Pattern 1: The Three Step Sequence

The three step sequence is the simplest reliable multi step pattern. Step one gathers material. Step two reasons about it. Step three produces the deliverable. This pattern works for analytical tasks, planning tasks, and many forms of structured creative work.

```
Three steps:  1. List the three main themes in the customer feedback below. 2.
For each theme, identify the most common underlying cause. 3. For each
underlying cause, propose one product change that would address it.  Produce
output as a markdown table with columns Theme, Cause, Proposed Change.
```

Pattern 2: The Diverge and Converge

This pattern starts wide and narrows. Step one generates many options. Step two narrows to the strongest few. Step three develops one in detail. The diverge and converge pattern is well suited to brainstorming followed by selection followed by execution.

```
Three steps:  1. Generate ten possible names for our new product line of organic
teas. 2. Of those ten, choose the three strongest, and explain why each is a
strong fit for our brand. 3. For the strongest of the three, write a one
paragraph rationale and propose a tagline.
```

Pattern 3: The Critique and Improve

This pattern produces output, then critiques it, then improves it. Step one drafts. Step two evaluates. Step three revises. The pattern produces higher quality output because the second step surfaces issues the AI would otherwise have skipped.

```
Three steps:  1. Write a 200 word company update about our recent product
launch. 2. Critique the draft you just wrote against these criteria: clarity,
brevity, accuracy, and warmth. Identify the top two weaknesses. 3. Rewrite the
draft to address those weaknesses. Show the revised version.
```

Pattern 4: The Multi Audience Tailoring

This pattern produces variants for different audiences. Step one drafts a base version. Steps two through four tailor it for specific audiences. The pattern is useful when the same content needs to reach multiple groups with different vocabulary and emphasis.

```
Four steps:  1. Draft a 150 word announcement of the policy change. 2. Tailor
the announcement for the engineering team, emphasizing operational implications.
3. Tailor the announcement for the marketing team, emphasizing customer
messaging. 4. Tailor the announcement for the executive team, emphasizing
strategic context.  Produce all four versions clearly labeled.
```

Where Multi Step Prompts Break Down

Multi step prompts have limits. Several signs indicate you are pushing too far.

- Steps blur together in the output. The AI produces a single response that does not clearly distinguish the stages.
- Later steps get visibly less attention. The first step is detailed, the last step is rushed.
- Earlier steps fade from the AI's reasoning. By step five, the AI seems to have forgotten what step one produced.
- The output exceeds the token budget, causing truncation.
- Iteration becomes hard. You cannot adjust step three without affecting everything else.

When you encounter these signs, the fix is to break the multi step prompt into separate prompts. Run step one. Review the output. Send step two. Review again. Continue. The conversation becomes a chain of focused interactions rather than one giant request. The output quality often improves dramatically with this restructuring. Chapter 7 covers prompt chaining in more depth.

4.13 Pattern Combinations and Personal Style

Section 4.6 mentioned that patterns can combine. This expansion explores how skilled prompt writers develop a personal style by mixing patterns according to the demands of each task. Personal style emerges from intentional practice, not from copying others.

The Role Plus Format Combination

One of the most useful combinations is role plus format. The role sets the perspective. The format constrains the structure. Together they produce output that has both the right voice and the right shape.

```
Act as a senior product manager at a B2B SaaS company. Produce a quarterly
review of these features as a markdown table with columns Feature, Status, Risk,
and Next Quarter Plan.
```

Notice how the role drives the substance, what a product manager would notice, and the format drives the structure. Either alone would be useful. Together they are stronger than the sum.

The Few Shot Plus Multi Step Combination

Another powerful combination is few shot plus multi step. Few shot examples teach the AI a custom pattern. Multi step structure breaks complex work into stages. The combination teaches the AI both the pattern and the process.

```
I will give you customer reviews to process. For each review, perform these
three steps:  1. Categorize the review as Positive, Negative, or Mixed. 2.
Identify the single most important customer concern. 3. Suggest a one sentence
response to the customer.  Here are two examples of correct output:  Review:
"The app is great but it crashes too often." Category: Mixed Concern: App
stability problems. Response: Thanks for the feedback. Stability is our top
engineering priority this quarter.  Review: "I cannot believe how good the
support team was." Category: Positive Concern: None, the customer is praising
support. Response: We are so glad to hear this. The support team will love
seeing this.  Now process these new reviews: ...
```

This kind of combined prompt produces consistent, structured output across many inputs because it teaches both the pattern (through examples) and the process (through steps). Building these combinations is part of growing into a more sophisticated prompt writer.

Developing Personal Style

Style emerges from practice. As you write more prompts, certain combinations will feel natural to you. You will reach for the role plus format combo for analytical tasks. You will reach for the few shot plus multi step combo for processing pipelines. You will reach for the diverge and converge for creative explorations. Each writer's style ends up slightly different, shaped by the kinds of work they do most often.

Resist the urge to standardize too early. Try many combinations. Notice what works for your kinds of tasks. Over time, your style will settle, but it should settle around what genuinely works for you, not around what someone else's style book recommends. Personal style, earned through experience, is one of the deepest assets a prompt writer can develop.

> **From Patterns to Style**
>
> Patterns are the alphabet. Style is the writing. Knowing the patterns is necessary but not sufficient. Combining them with judgment, attuned to your own tasks and aesthetic, is what separates good prompt writers from excellent ones.

4.14 The Pattern Decision Tree

With several design patterns now in your toolkit, the question becomes which to choose for which task. The decision tree below provides a starting framework. Walk through the questions in order. Each yes or no leads you toward a pattern that fits.

Question 1: Is the Task a Single Quick Answer?

If yes, use a direct prompt. The capital of France is Paris. No need for elaborate setup.

If no, continue.

Question 2: Does the Task Have a Specific Action and Input?

If yes, use an instruction based prompt. Translate this paragraph. Summarize this article. The structure is action plus input.

If no, continue.

Question 3: Would a Specific Perspective Improve the Output?

If yes, use a role based prompt. Acting as a senior copy editor, review this draft. The role focuses the output.

If no, continue.

Question 4: Is the Output Format Critical to Usability?

If yes, use a format driven prompt. Produce a markdown table with columns Name, Status, Risk. The format shapes both presentation and reasoning.

If no, continue.

Question 5: Does the Task Have Multiple Sequential Stages?

If yes, use a multi step prompt. First do X. Then do Y. Finally do Z. The structure breaks complex work into manageable parts.

If no, return to question one. Most tasks fit one of the patterns above.

When Multiple Patterns Apply

Many real tasks fit multiple patterns. The decision tree helps you find the most prominent fit, but skilled prompters often combine patterns. Acting as a senior strategist (role), produce a market analysis (instruction) as a markdown table (format) following these steps (multi step). The combination is often more powerful than any single pattern alone.

4.15 Pattern Mistakes and How to Avoid Them

Each design pattern has characteristic ways of going wrong. Knowing them in advance helps you avoid them when applying the pattern.

Direct Prompt Mistakes

The main mistake with direct prompts is using them when the task actually needs more structure. A direct prompt for a complex task produces output that lacks the structure complex output needs. The fix is to upgrade to instruction based or multi step when the task is non trivial.

Instruction Based Prompt Mistakes

The main mistake with instruction based prompts is stacking too many instructions in one prompt. The AI rations attention and produces partial coverage of each. The fix is to do one instruction per prompt, or to chain prompts so each step is focused.

Role Based Prompt Mistakes

The main mistake with role based prompts is choosing a role that does not fit the task. Acting as a Shakespearean playwright, write a customer support email is funny but not useful. The role should match the task, not provide novelty for its own sake.

Format Driven Prompt Mistakes

The main mistake with format driven prompts is forcing content into a format that does not suit it. Forcing flowing prose into a table fragments the prose. Forcing structured data into prose loses precision. The fix is to match the format to the content shape.

Multi Step Prompt Mistakes

The main mistake with multi step prompts is having steps that do not actually depend on each other. Independent steps in one prompt are just three prompts pretending to be one. The fix is to phrase later steps so they explicitly build on earlier output.

4.16 Pattern Selection in Practice: Five Scenarios

To make pattern selection concrete, here are five scenarios with the recommended pattern and a brief example.

Scenario 1: Quick Factual Lookup

Task: Confirm the population of Toronto.

Pattern: Direct prompt.

Example: What is the population of Toronto?

Scenario 2: Document Transformation

Task: Convert a long technical document into a one page executive summary.

Pattern: Instruction based with format driven elements.

Example: Summarize the document below into a one page executive summary. Use these labeled sections: Bottom Line, Key Findings, Risks, Recommendations. Length: 250 words total.

Scenario 3: Specialist Analysis

Task: Get a security focused analysis of code.

Pattern: Role based with format driven elements.

Example: Acting as a senior security engineer, review the code below. Identify any security issues. For each issue, provide a labeled item with: Severity, Description, Suggested fix.

Scenario 4: Structured Comparison

Task: Compare three options for a decision.

Pattern: Format driven.

Example: Compare these three vendor options. Produce a markdown table with columns Vendor, Cost, Time to Implement, Key Strengths, Key Risks. Then add a one paragraph recommendation.

Scenario 5: Complex Strategic Workflow

Task: Plan a quarterly strategy from a set of inputs.

Pattern: Multi step combined with role based and format driven elements.

Example: Acting as a senior strategy consultant, walk through these steps. Step 1: Read the inputs below and identify the three biggest opportunities and three biggest risks. Step 2: For each opportunity, propose two strategic moves we could make this quarter. Step 3: For each risk, propose one mitigation. Step 4: Synthesize into a one page strategy memo with sections Opportunities, Risks, and Recommended Quarter Plan.

The Pattern as Default

Most experienced prompt writers have a default pattern they reach for first, then deviate from when the task warrants. Direct prompts for quick lookups. Instruction based for everyday tasks. Role plus format for analytical work. Multi step for complex strategic workflows. Build your own defaults through practice.

4.17 An Extended Persona Library by Industry

Section 4.10 introduced a library of personas. Below is an extended list organized by industry, with notes on what each persona does best. Use these as starting points and adapt to your specific situations.

Healthcare and Medical

- Family medicine physician explaining concepts to a worried patient. For: clear, gentle explanations of medical concepts.
- Hospital administrator reviewing operational efficiency. For: operational analysis, scheduling, throughput.
- Pharmacist explaining medication interactions. For: clear safety information, drug knowledge.
- Public health researcher writing for policy audiences. For: epidemiological reasoning, policy implications.
- Medical writer producing patient education materials. For: accessible health content, plain language.

Education

- Elementary school teacher explaining a concept to nine year olds. For: vivid metaphors, simple vocabulary, engagement.
- Middle school teacher creating discussion prompts. For: open ended questions, scaffolded thinking.

- High school teacher preparing students for standardized exams. For: structured study, test taking strategies.
- College professor writing a syllabus. For: course design, learning objectives, assessment planning.
- Educational researcher reviewing pedagogical literature. For: synthesizing research, identifying patterns.

Legal and Compliance

- Contract lawyer reviewing a draft agreement. For: identifying risk, suggesting language.
- Regulatory compliance officer in a small business. For: practical compliance steps, prioritization.
- Privacy lawyer explaining data protection. For: clear explanations of complex regulations.
- Litigation attorney reviewing case strategy. For: argument development, witness preparation.
- Paralegal preparing case summaries. For: factual extraction, organization.

Finance

- Personal financial advisor for early career professionals. For: practical money advice, accessible explanations.
- Wealth manager for high net worth individuals. For: sophisticated investment, tax strategy.
- Corporate treasurer managing cash flow. For: working capital, financial planning.
- Investment banker preparing pitch materials. For: deal structure, valuation rationale.
- Compliance officer in a financial services firm. For: regulatory reporting, audit preparation.

Retail and Hospitality

- Independent retail store owner. For: small business decisions, customer experience.
- Restaurant manager handling operations. For: menu planning, staff scheduling.
- Hotel general manager focused on guest experience. For: service standards, problem resolution.
- E commerce category manager. For: assortment decisions, pricing, promotional strategy.
- Customer experience researcher. For: journey mapping, pain point identification.

Nonprofit and Public Sector

- Executive director of a small nonprofit. For: fundraising, board relations, strategic planning.
- Grant writer for educational programs. For: persuasive proposals, impact framing.
- City planner advising on zoning. For: balancing competing interests, public input.
- Public communications officer. For: clear messaging on policy.
- Volunteer coordinator. For: recruitment, engagement, recognition.

4.18 Pattern Combinations: Five Detailed Examples

Section 4.13 introduced pattern combinations. Below are five detailed examples of effective combinations for different kinds of work, with notes on what each combination does well.

Combination 1: Role Plus Multi Step

```
Acting as a senior product manager at a B2B SaaS company, walk through the
following four steps to evaluate this feature request from a customer.  Step 1:
Identify the underlying problem the customer is trying to solve, distinct from
their proposed solution. Step 2: Estimate how many customers in our base would
benefit from solving this problem. Step 3: Brainstorm three possible solutions,
ranging from minimal to ambitious. Step 4: Recommend which solution, if any,
fits in next quarter's roadmap, with one paragraph of rationale.  [Customer
feature request below]
```

Why this combination works: the role activates product manager judgment. The multi step structure prevents the common failure of jumping to solutions before understanding the underlying problem. Together they produce thoughtful, prioritized analysis.

Combination 2: Few Shot Plus Format Driven

```
Categorize each customer email using these labels: Bug, Feature Request,
Confusion, Compliment.  Examples:  Email: "The export button does not work on
Safari." Label: Bug  Email: "It would be great if you could add a dark mode
option." Label: Feature Request  Email: "I cannot figure out how to share a
board with my team." Label: Confusion  Email: "Your team's responsiveness is the
best I have experienced from any vendor." Label: Compliment  Now categorize the
following emails. Output as a markdown table with columns Email Number, Email
Excerpt, Label, Confidence (high or low).
```

Why this combination works: the few shot examples teach the category boundaries. The format driven output makes the results consistently structured and easy to consume. Together they produce reliable, scannable categorization.

Combination 3: Role Plus Format Driven Plus Multi Step

```
Acting as an experienced UX researcher, follow these three steps to synthesize
the user interview data below.  Step 1: Identify recurring themes across the
interviews, with at least three quotes supporting each theme. Step 2: For each
theme, propose a hypothesis about its underlying cause. Step 3: For each
hypothesis, suggest one specific research question for the next round of
interviews.  Produce output as a markdown table with columns Theme, Supporting
Quotes, Hypothesis, Next Research Question.  [Interview transcripts below]
```

Why this combination works: the role activates UX research judgment. The multi step structure ensures themes are evidenced before hypotheses are formed. The format driven output makes the synthesis usable by the rest of the team.

Combination 4: Direct Plus Critique Loop

```
Step 1: Write a 100 word product description for our new noise canceling
headphones.  Step 2: Critique the description you just wrote against these
criteria: clarity of value proposition, emotional resonance, distinctiveness
from competitors, fit for the target audience (commuters and remote workers).
Step 3: Rewrite the description to address the critique. Show only the final
version.
```

Why this combination works: the AI's first attempt at copy is often generic. The critique step surfaces specific weaknesses. The rewrite addresses them. The final output is meaningfully better than what a single direct prompt would produce.

Combination 5: Source Bound Plus Format Driven Plus Uncertainty Flag

```
Use only the information in the document below to answer the questions. Do not
invent facts or numbers. If a question cannot be answered from the document,
mark the answer as Not in source.  [Document below]  Produce a markdown table
with columns Question, Answer, Confidence (high, medium, low), and Source (page
or section reference if available).  Questions: 1. What is the company's
reported revenue for the most recent fiscal year? 2. How many employees does the
company have? 3. What is the company's stated growth strategy for the next two
years? 4. What are the company's three largest customer segments? 5. What is the
company's debt to equity ratio?
```

Why this combination works: source binding prevents fabrication. The structured format produces consistent, scannable output. The uncertainty flag invites honest gaps. Together they produce factual extraction that is both rigorous and useful.

Chapter 5: Zero Shot and Few Shot Prompting

In Chapters 3 and 4, we built and patterned prompts. Now we turn to a deeper question. How do you teach the AI what kind of output you want, especially when the task is unusual or your standards are specific? The answer lies in two foundational techniques known as zero shot prompting and few shot prompting. Together, they form one of the most powerful pairs of techniques in the prompting toolkit.

These terms come from machine learning research, but the ideas behind them are intuitive. Zero shot prompting means asking the AI to perform a task with no examples provided. Few shot prompting means asking the AI to perform a task while showing it a few examples of the kind of input and output you want. Each has its place. Knowing when to use which, and how to design the examples that make few shot prompting work, separates competent prompt writers from advanced ones.

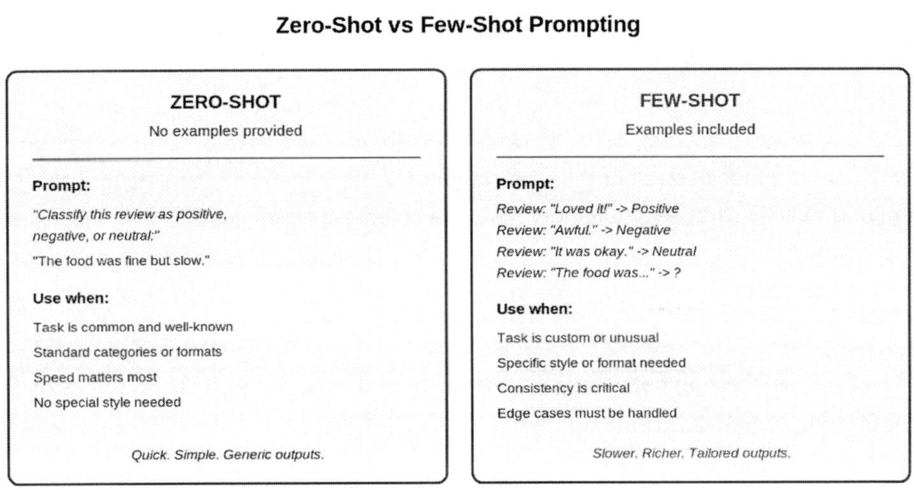

Figure 5.1: Zero shot and few shot prompting compared side by side.

5.1 What Is Zero Shot Prompting?

Zero shot prompting is the kind of prompting we have been doing throughout the book so far. You give the AI an instruction and any necessary context, and you ask it to produce an output. You provide no examples. The AI relies entirely on its training and on your instruction to figure out what kind of output you want.

Examples of zero shot prompts include: classify this customer review as positive, negative, or neutral; summarize this article in three sentences; translate this paragraph to Spanish; write a five line poem about autumn. In each of these, no examples are provided. The AI is expected to know how to perform the task because the task itself is common in its training data.

Why Zero Shot Often Works

Zero shot prompting works because modern AI models have been trained on enormous amounts of text covering an enormous range of tasks. They have seen countless reviews classified by sentiment, countless articles summarized, countless translations between major languages, and countless poems on countless themes. When you ask for any of these things, the AI does not need an example. It already knows the shape.

This is why zero shot prompts work so well for common tasks. The AI has a strong prior expectation of what the task involves and produces output that fits that prior. As long as the task is one the AI has effectively seen many times before, zero shot is fast, simple, and effective.

When Zero Shot Falls Short

Zero shot prompting begins to struggle when the task is uncommon, the format is unusual, or your standards are specific. If you ask the AI to classify customer reviews into the three categories of fan, frustrated, and undecided rather than the standard positive, negative, and neutral, the AI may not understand exactly what each category means without examples. If you ask the AI to follow a strict idiosyncratic format, the AI may pick a similar but slightly different format. If your tone preferences differ from the typical patterns the AI has learned, the AI may not match them on the first try.

In all of these cases, the gap between what you want and what the AI defaults to is exactly the gap that few shot prompting bridges.

5.2 When to Use Zero Shot Prompting

Zero shot prompting is the right choice in several situations.

1. The task is common and well established. Sentiment classification, summarization, translation between major languages, and standard kinds of writing are all well covered.
2. The output format is conventional. Bulleted lists, paragraphs, and standard tables are familiar shapes.
3. Speed matters more than absolute precision. Zero shot prompts are quicker to write because they do not require crafting examples.

4. You are exploring possibilities. When you do not yet know exactly what kind of output you want, starting zero shot lets you see the AI's default before you decide whether to refine.
5. You want generic output rather than personalized output. If your goal is a generally good summary or translation, zero shot is fine. If your goal is one in your specific voice, examples help.

In short, zero shot is the default for most everyday prompting. It is fast, easy, and often sufficient. Reach for few shot when the task or your standards exceed what zero shot can comfortably handle.

5.3 Few Shot Prompting With Examples

Few shot prompting is a technique where you include several examples of input and desired output within the prompt itself. The AI uses those examples to infer the pattern you want and applies that pattern to new input. The examples teach the AI without any model retraining. They simply guide the AI's response in the moment.

A simple few shot prompt for a custom classification task might look like this:

```
Classify each customer review using exactly one of these labels: Fan,
Frustrated, Undecided.  Review: "This is the best service I have ever used. Tell
everyone you know." Label: Fan  Review: "I have been calling for a week and no
one returns my call." Label: Frustrated  Review: "It is okay. I have not made up
my mind yet." Label: Undecided  Review: "I love the design but the shipping took
forever." Label:
```

The AI sees three examples that establish the pattern and then encounters a fourth review with no label. It will produce a label that fits the pattern, even though the labels Fan, Frustrated, and Undecided are not standard sentiment categories. The examples have effectively taught the AI a custom classification task on the fly.

5.4 Designing Effective Examples

The power of few shot prompting depends almost entirely on the quality of the examples. Good examples produce good results. Sloppy examples produce inconsistent results. The good news is that designing effective examples is a skill that can be learned, and the principles are surprisingly simple.

Principle One: Examples Should Be Clear

Each example should be unambiguous. The input should be a clear instance of the kind of input you expect. The output should be a clear instance of the kind of output you want. Avoid borderline cases in your examples, since they teach the AI mixed signals. Save the borderline cases for the test, not for the training.

Principle Two: Examples Should Be Diverse

If your examples are all similar, the AI may overfit to that narrow pattern. Mix the examples so they cover different shapes the input can take. For a classification task, include examples of each class. For a transformation task, include examples that vary in length, tone, or topic. Diversity in examples produces robustness in output.

Principle Three: Format Examples Consistently

Use the same format for every example. If the first example uses Review and Label, every example should use Review and Label. If the first example separates input and output with a colon, every example should use a colon. Inconsistent formatting confuses the AI and produces unpredictable output. Pick a format and stick to it.

Principle Four: Order Matters

The order in which examples appear can subtly influence the AI's interpretation. Examples near the end of the prompt tend to weigh slightly more in the AI's pattern matching, especially when the prompt is long. Place your most representative examples last if you can. Place your most diverse or edge case examples in the middle to demonstrate range without anchoring on them too heavily.

Principle Five: Three to Five Examples Is Usually Enough

There is a temptation to provide many examples, sometimes ten or more. In most cases, this does not help and may hurt. Three to five well chosen examples are usually enough to establish a clear pattern. Beyond that, you risk crowding the prompt, distracting from the actual task, and introducing inconsistencies.

Few Shot Design Checklist

Are your examples clear instances? Are they diverse? Are they formatted consistently? Are they in a thoughtful order? Are there enough but not too many? Each yes brings your few shot prompt closer to its full potential.

5.5 Comparing Outputs With and Without Examples

To make the value of few shot prompting concrete, let us walk through a side by side comparison. The task is to extract a particular kind of structured insight from a paragraph of customer feedback.

Zero Shot Version

```
Read the customer feedback below and identify the customer's primary concern.
Feedback: "I love the new app, but the checkout process feels clunky. I have to
tap through three screens just to confirm my order."
```

The AI will likely produce a reasonable answer. Something like, the customer's primary concern is that the checkout process is clunky and requires too many steps. Useful, but generic. The output is prose. The structure is invented. The depth is whatever the AI feels appropriate.

Few Shot Version

```
Read each piece of customer feedback and extract the customer's primary concern
using this format. Use exactly two fields: Issue and Suggested Fix.  Feedback:
"The app crashes every time I try to upload a photo." Issue: App crashes during
photo upload. Suggested Fix: Investigate and resolve the photo upload bug.
Feedback: "Notifications come in at 3 AM and wake me up." Issue: Notifications
arrive at unwanted hours. Suggested Fix: Add quiet hours preference setting.
Feedback: "I cannot find the export option anywhere." Issue: Export feature is
hard to discover. Suggested Fix: Make export option more visible in the menu.
Feedback: "I love the new app, but the checkout process feels clunky. I have to
tap through three screens just to confirm my order." Issue:
```

Now the AI has a clear template. It will produce something like Issue: Checkout process is too long, requiring three screens to confirm order. Suggested Fix: Streamline checkout flow into a single screen confirmation. Same input. Far more useful output. The examples taught the AI exactly what shape, depth, and orientation you wanted.

This is the heart of few shot prompting. By showing the AI a small number of examples, you can teach it almost any structured pattern, custom classification, idiosyncratic format, particular voice, or specific level of analysis. It is one of the highest leverage techniques in the entire field of prompt engineering.

5.6 Common Mistakes With Few Shot Prompting

Few shot prompting is powerful, but it is also easy to misuse. Several common mistakes can undermine its effectiveness.

1. Examples that contradict each other. If your examples disagree about the desired pattern, the AI cannot resolve the conflict and will produce inconsistent output.

2. Examples that are too narrow. If all your examples cover one corner of the input space, the AI may fail on input that lies outside that corner.
3. Examples that are too long. If each example is a paragraph and you have five of them, the prompt becomes bloated. Keep examples concise.
4. Examples that include the answer to the test case. This sounds obvious, but it happens often when reusing prompts. Make sure your test input is genuinely new.
5. Format drift in the test case. If you use Review for examples and review for the test case, the AI may produce output in a different format. Be consistent.

Avoiding these mistakes is largely a matter of careful proofreading. Read your prompt aloud. Check that the examples agree, that they cover the relevant input shapes, and that the format is consistent throughout.

5.7 Choosing Between Zero Shot and Few Shot

With both techniques in your toolkit, the question becomes when to reach for which. The decision usually hinges on two factors. How common is the task? And how specific are your output standards?

Task Commonness	Standards Specificity	Recommended Technique
Common	Standard	Zero shot. Fast and effective.
Common	Specific	Few shot. Examples lock in your standards.
Uncommon	Standard	Few shot. Examples teach the unusual task.
Uncommon	Specific	Few shot, with extra care in example design.

In practice, most beginners under use few shot prompting. They reach for it only after several zero shot attempts disappoint them. A more efficient habit is to ask, before writing the prompt, whether the task or the standards justify the upfront effort of crafting examples. If yes, start with few shot. If no, start with zero shot. This decision saves time on average.

5.8 Chapter Recap

This chapter introduced two foundational techniques: zero shot prompting and few shot prompting. Let us consolidate the key ideas.

- Zero shot prompting asks the AI to perform a task with no examples, relying on the AI's training to know the task.
- Zero shot works well for common tasks with conventional formats and standard expectations.
- Few shot prompting includes a few examples of input and desired output within the prompt, teaching the AI a custom pattern.
- Effective examples are clear, diverse, consistently formatted, thoughtfully ordered, and limited to three to five.
- Few shot is the right choice when the task is uncommon, the format is unusual, or your standards are specific.
- The same input often produces dramatically different output in zero shot versus few shot, with few shot generally producing more useful structured results.

Practice Exercise

This single comparison tends to convert prompt writers into believers in the power of examples.

1. Pick a task you have struggled to get satisfying output for using zero shot prompting. Choose a real task, not a synthetic one.
2. Run a clean zero shot version of the prompt first and save the output.
3. Design a few shot prompt for the same task with three to five well chosen examples. Make the examples diverse, consistently formatted, and ordered logically.
4. Run the few shot version and save the output.
5. Compare the two outputs side by side, paying attention to format, depth, and consistency.

Most prompt writers are surprised by how much the few shot version improves the output, especially in format consistency. The lesson sticks because you generated the evidence yourself.

5.9 Zero Shot Prompting in Depth

Section 5.1 introduced zero shot prompting. This expansion looks at when zero shot prompts succeed beautifully, when they quietly fail, and how to recognize the difference before you have wasted iterations on a doomed approach.

Hidden Successes of Zero Shot Prompting

Zero shot prompts work well in surprisingly many situations because the underlying tasks are so common in the AI's training data. Categorizing customer feedback into positive, negative, and neutral. Translating between major languages. Summarizing news articles. Writing standard business emails. Producing simple code in popular languages. Naming things in conventional patterns. All of these are heavily represented in training data, and the AI has effectively done them millions of times before. Your zero shot prompt taps into that latent capacity, and the output reflects it.

Recognizing tasks that are well covered by zero shot saves you the effort of crafting examples when none are needed. The signal is that the task feels common, that you can imagine many other people doing the same task, and that there is a clear mainstream way to perform it. When all three conditions are true, zero shot is a strong default.

Hidden Failures of Zero Shot Prompting

Zero shot prompts fail more subtly than they succeed. The output looks competent but does not match what you specifically wanted. Several failure patterns repeat.

1. Format drift. The AI produces a list when you wanted a paragraph, or paragraphs when you wanted a list, because it picked a default that does not match your taste.
2. Tone drift. The AI produces a default professional tone when you wanted something warmer or punchier, because the default is what training data has most of.
3. Coverage drift. The AI covers some aspects of a topic but not the ones you cared about, because it cannot read your mind about which dimensions matter.
4. Length drift. The AI produces a longer or shorter response than fits your need, because it has its own sense of what feels appropriate.
5. Specificity drift. The AI produces general statements when you wanted specifics, or specifics when you wanted overview, because the level of granularity is left implicit.

In each of these patterns, the output is not wrong. It is misaligned with what you specifically wanted. The cure is either to add tighter constraints to the zero shot prompt or to upgrade to few shot. Knowing which to choose is part of the skill.

Diagnosing a Failed Zero Shot

When zero shot output does not satisfy you, ask yourself a single diagnostic question. What about the output, specifically, does not match what I wanted? The answer points to the dimension you should have constrained more tightly. Format mismatch points to format constraints. Tone mismatch points to tonal constraints. Coverage mismatch points to context. Length mismatch points to length constraints. Specificity mismatch points to either format or examples.

This diagnosis is faster than blindly rewriting the prompt. It tells you what to add, not just that something needs adding. With practice, the diagnosis becomes near instant. You read the output, identify the dimension that drifted, and make a targeted addition. The next attempt is often dramatically better.

5.10 The Mechanics of Few Shot Learning

Section 5.3 introduced few shot prompting. This expansion examines what is actually happening when the AI processes few shot examples, and how to use that understanding to design more effective examples.

Why Examples Work

When you include examples in a prompt, the AI is not learning in any deep sense. Its weights are not changing. What is happening is something more subtle. The AI is using the examples as the most recent context it has seen, and that context strongly influences the patterns it expects in the next response. Recent context weighs heavily in the AI's predictions. Examples are recent context. Examples are therefore disproportionately influential.

This means that examples are most effective when they are placed near the end of the prompt, when they are clearly delimited from instructions, and when the actual test case immediately follows the examples in the same format. The AI then continues the pattern naturally, producing output that fits the established shape.

Designing Examples That Teach the Right Thing

Each example you include teaches the AI multiple things at once. The format of the input. The format of the output. The relationship between input and output. The level of detail in the output. The tone of the output. The length of the output. The vocabulary of the output. All of these are absorbed simultaneously.

This means that subtle inconsistencies in your examples can teach the AI the wrong thing. If two examples have different output lengths, the AI may produce inconsistent lengths. If three examples have different formats, the AI may pick whichever feels most plausible for each test case. Consistency across examples is critical, and consistency in subtle dimensions matters as much as consistency in obvious ones.

The Trade Off Between Diversity and Consistency

Examples should be diverse enough to cover the input shapes you expect but consistent enough to teach a single coherent pattern. The trade off is real. Too consistent and the AI overfits to a narrow pattern. Too diverse and the AI cannot extract a single pattern at all.

A useful guideline is to keep the format identical across all examples but vary the content of the inputs. Same format, different content. This produces examples that teach the format clearly while exposing the AI to a range of inputs. The AI learns to apply the format to new inputs of similar diversity.

5.11 Worked Examples of Few Shot Design

Theory becomes useful when grounded in worked examples. Below are three detailed walkthroughs of designing few shot prompts for different kinds of tasks. Each shows the design decisions and the resulting prompt.

Worked Example 1: Custom Categorization

Task. Categorize customer support tickets into one of four custom categories that do not match any standard taxonomy: Bug, Confusion, Feature Request, and Complaint. The challenge is that the AI does not know exactly what counts as Confusion versus Bug, since both could involve broken behavior. Examples disambiguate.

```
Categorize each customer support ticket using exactly one of these four labels:
Bug, Confusion, Feature Request, Complaint.  Definitions: - Bug: Something that
does not work as designed. - Confusion: The customer misunderstands how
something is supposed to work. - Feature Request: The customer wants a
capability we do not currently offer. - Complaint: The customer is unhappy but
not reporting a specific defect or asking for a feature.  Examples:  Ticket: "I
clicked save and my work disappeared. I tried again and it happened again."
Label: Bug  Ticket: "Why does the export only give me a CSV? I need a PDF for my
boss." Label: Feature Request  Ticket: "I cannot find the dashboard. I logged in
and there is just a sidebar." Label: Confusion  Ticket: "Your service is way too
expensive for what you offer. Disappointed." Label: Complaint  Now categorize:
Ticket: "The notification settings have no way to silence weekend pings, which I
never want." Label:
```

Notice the design decisions. The definitions are explicit, since the categories are custom. Each example illustrates a different category, ensuring all four are represented. The format of input and output is identical across examples. The test ticket is added in the same format. The AI will produce a label that fits the pattern, and because each category has a clear example, the label will be reliable.

Worked Example 2: Style Transfer

Task. Rewrite product descriptions in the voice of a specific brand. The brand voice is warm, slightly playful, and uses short sentences. The challenge is that warm, playful, and short are vague. Examples make the voice concrete.

```
Rewrite each product description in our brand voice. Match the rhythm,
vocabulary, and tone of the examples below.  Examples:  Original: "This
insulated water bottle keeps liquids cold for 24 hours and hot for 12 hours."
Rewritten: "Cold drinks stay cold. All day. Hot drinks stay hot too. Some
```

```
bottles try harder. This is one of them."  Original: "Our notebook has 200 pages
of premium paper, ideal for journaling and note taking." Rewritten: "Two hundred
pages. Real good paper. The kind that takes ink without sulking. Ready when you
are."  Original: "This backpack features ergonomic straps and waterproof
compartments for all weather use." Rewritten: "Built for shoulders that walk a
lot. Built for rain that does not care about your stuff. The straps know. The
pockets know. Now you do too."  Now rewrite:  Original: "Our pen uses gel ink
for smooth writing and comes in twelve colors." Rewritten:
```

Notice that the examples teach a very specific voice that no amount of verbal description could capture. Sentence fragments. Repetition for rhythm. Direct address. Small confidences. The AI absorbs all of this through pattern matching against the examples and produces output in the same voice. This kind of style transfer is extremely difficult through verbal direction alone but routine through few shot examples.

Worked Example 3: Structured Data Extraction

Task. Extract structured information from messy, varied customer emails. The output must be JSON with specific keys. The challenge is that the input is unstructured prose and the output must be reliable structured data.

```
Extract structured information from each customer email. Output as JSON with
these keys: customer_name, request_type, urgency (high, medium, low), and
summary (one sentence).  Examples:  Email: "Hi, this is Sarah from Acme Corp. We
need help configuring SSO for our new hire onboarding next Monday. Can someone
get back to us today?" Output: {   "customer_name": "Sarah",   "request_type":
"SSO configuration",   "urgency": "high",   "summary": "Sarah from Acme needs
SSO configured before next Monday's onboarding." }  Email: "Hello, my name is
Marcus. I was wondering if your platform supports SAML integration. No rush,
just researching for a future project." Output: {   "customer_name": "Marcus",
"request_type": "SAML inquiry",   "urgency": "low",   "summary": "Marcus is
researching SAML support for a future project." }  Email: "Tara here. The
dashboard has been loading slowly for two days for our entire team. Twenty users
are affected. Please escalate." Output: {   "customer_name": "Tara",
"request_type": "performance issue",   "urgency": "high",   "summary": "Tara
reports two days of slow dashboard loading affecting 20 users." }  Now extract:
Email: "Hey, this is Devon. I noticed the export button is not visible on
mobile. Whenever you get a chance to look into it would be great." Output:
```

This kind of structured extraction is one of the highest leverage uses of few shot prompting. The examples teach the AI both the format and the judgment, urgency assessment, summary length, and how to label request types in your specific way. The output becomes consistent enough to feed directly into other software systems.

5.12 Pitfalls in Few Shot Design

Few shot prompts work brilliantly when designed well and fail in characteristic ways when designed poorly. Below are the most common pitfalls and how to avoid them.

Pitfall 1: Examples That Conflict

If two examples teach inconsistent patterns, the AI cannot resolve the conflict. The output may follow one example for some test cases and another for others, producing inconsistent output. The fix is to audit your examples for conflicts. Are the formats truly identical? Are the output lengths truly comparable? Are the judgment calls truly aligned? Conflicts often hide in subtle dimensions like punctuation or capitalization.

Pitfall 2: Edge Case Examples

Beginners sometimes pick edge cases as examples, thinking they will teach robustness. Edge cases instead teach the AI that the task is mostly about edge cases, biasing output. Use clear, central examples for most of your few shot prompts. If you need to handle edge cases, add them as additional examples that supplement, not replace, the central ones.

Pitfall 3: Overlapping Examples

If two examples are very similar to each other, you have used your example budget on near duplicates. The AI learns one pattern from two examples instead of two patterns. Mix your examples so each one teaches something different. Diversity in examples produces robustness in output.

Pitfall 4: Unrealistic Examples

Sometimes examples are crafted so beautifully that they do not match real input. The AI learns a pattern that fits clean examples but not messy real data. Use examples that look like the real inputs you will be processing, including imperfections like typos, vague phrasing, or unusual structure if those will appear in production.

Pitfall 5: Too Many Examples

Some users include ten, fifteen, or twenty examples thinking more is better. Beyond about five, additional examples often hurt by crowding the prompt and introducing inconsistencies. Three to five well chosen examples almost always outperform a longer list.

The Five Example Limit

If you find yourself wanting to add a sixth or seventh example, ask whether each existing example is genuinely teaching something different. Often you can replace two similar examples with one stronger one. Quality over quantity, every time.

5.13 The Scope of Few Shot Capabilities

Few shot prompting is more powerful than most beginners realize. Below is a survey of the kinds of tasks where few shot consistently outperforms zero shot, with notes on what specifically the examples are teaching.

Task Type	What Examples Teach	Why Few Shot Wins
Custom classification	The category boundaries.	Categories you invent are not in training data.
Style transfer	The voice through pattern matching.	Voice is hard to describe verbally.
Structured extraction	The exact output schema.	Verbal description of JSON is fragile.
Domain specific reasoning	How experts in your domain reason.	General reasoning may not match your domain.
Complex formatting	The exact layout you want.	Format details are hard to describe in words.
Custom labeling	Your specific tagging scheme.	Labels you invent need definition by example.
Brand voice writing	Your specific brand register.	Brand voice is built from many subtle choices.
Edge case handling	What to do in unusual situations.	Examples make boundary cases concrete.

Task Type	What Examples Teach	Why Few Shot Wins
Multi step reasoning patterns	The exact reasoning chain you prefer.	Reasoning style is hard to specify verbally.
Quality calibration	What you consider good or bad output.	Quality bars are subjective and need anchoring.

This range gives you a sense of how broadly applicable few shot prompting is. Whenever the task involves either custom standards or hard to describe qualities, few shot is likely to outperform zero shot. The investment in crafting examples pays back many times in output quality and consistency.

5.14 The Practice Loop for Few Shot Mastery

Few shot prompting is a skill that improves through deliberate practice. A good practice loop has four steps.

1. Pick a task you have struggled with using zero shot. The frustration is the signal that few shot might help.
2. Design three to five examples by hand. Make them clear, diverse, and consistent. Resist the urge to use the AI to generate examples for itself, since that may bake in the same patterns you are trying to override.
3. Run the few shot prompt. Compare the output to your zero shot baseline. Note specifically what improved and what did not.
4. Refine your examples. Sometimes one example is doing more work than expected and others are redundant. Keep the strong ones, replace the weak ones.

Cycle through this loop a few times for each task you care about. Within a handful of iterations, you will have few shot prompts that produce reliable output for tasks that previously felt unreliable. The investment is small, the payoff is large, and the skill compounds across many future tasks.

5.15 Twelve Detailed Few Shot Templates

Few shot prompting becomes second nature when you have a stock of templates ready to deploy. Below are twelve detailed templates for tasks where few shot consistently outperforms zero shot. Each shows the pattern, examples, and notes on adaptation.

Template 1: Sentiment Classification With Custom Categories

```
Classify each piece of feedback using one of these custom labels: Loyal Fan, Frustrated Loyal, Neutral, At Risk, Detractor.  Definitions: - Loyal Fan: Strongly positive, indicates active advocacy. - Frustrated Loyal: Reports issues but signals continued commitment. - Neutral: No strong sentiment in either direction. - At Risk: Reports issues with signals of potential departure. - Detractor: Strongly negative, indicates likely churn.  Examples:  Feedback: "I have recommended this product to three colleagues." Label: Loyal Fan Feedback: "The new update broke our workflow but we are working around it." Label: Frustrated Loyal Feedback: "The tool does what it says." Label: Neutral Feedback: "We are evaluating alternatives this quarter." Label: At Risk Feedback: "Worst purchase decision we made all year." Label: Detractor  Now classify:  Feedback: "Customer support is great but the product itself is starting to feel dated." Label:
```

Template 2: Brand Voice Style Transfer

```
Rewrite each marketing message in our brand voice. Match the rhythm, vocabulary, and emotional register of the examples below.  Examples:  Original: "This planner has 200 pages and includes weekly and monthly views." Rewritten: "Two hundred pages. Real paper. Real space to think. Weekly and monthly. Built for people who plan and people who pretend to plan."  Original: "Our coffee subscription delivers fresh beans every two weeks." Rewritten: "Beans you actually want to grind. Delivered before you run out. Every two weeks. Roasted last week. Ready to make tomorrow morning bearable."  Original: "This water bottle has a temperature display." Rewritten: "It tells you the temperature. We did not invent thermodynamics, just a small useful screen on a nice bottle. You will probably check it more than you should."  Now rewrite:  Original: "Our backpack is waterproof and has padded laptop storage." Rewritten:
```

Template 3: Email Triage

```
Categorize each customer email by urgency and type. Output as JSON with keys urgency (high, medium, low) and type (Sales, Support, Billing, Other). Examples:  Email: "Our system is down. We need help immediately." Output: {"urgency": "high", "type": "Support"}  Email: "Can you tell me more about your enterprise pricing?" Output: {"urgency": "medium", "type": "Sales"}  Email: "I was charged twice this month." Output: {"urgency": "high", "type": "Billing"} Email: "Just wanted to say I really appreciate the team." Output: {"urgency": "low", "type": "Other"}  Now categorize:  Email: "My account login is not working when I try from mobile." Output:
```

Template 4: Meeting Notes To Action Items

```
Convert meeting notes into structured action items. Each action item must have an owner and due date if mentioned.  Examples:  Notes: "Discussed Q4 launch. Sarah will draft the press release by Friday. Marcus to review the website changes next Tuesday. We still need to decide on the launch event venue." Action items: - [Sarah] Draft press release. Due: Friday. - [Marcus] Review website changes. Due: next Tuesday. - [Unassigned] Decide launch event venue. Due: Not specified.  Notes: "Reviewed customer feedback. Everyone agreed the onboarding flow needs work. Devon volunteered to lead a redesign starting next week. Olivia will gather competitor examples by Wednesday."  Action items: - [Devon] Lead onboarding flow redesign. Due: starts next week. - [Olivia] Gather competitor onboarding examples. Due: Wednesday. - [All] Reviewed feedback indicating onboarding flow needs work. (Background, no owner.)  Now extract action items from these notes:  Notes: "Discussed budget for next quarter. Need to cut 10 percent. Priya will identify candidate cuts by next Monday. Asked Carlos to model the impact on hiring plans by mid month. Unresolved: whether to delay the office move."  Action items:
```

Template 5: Resume Bullet Improvement

```
Rewrite each resume bullet to be more impactful. Use this pattern: action verb, what was done, measurable outcome.  Examples:  Original: "Worked on the new website launch." Rewritten: "Led the website redesign launch, increasing organic traffic by 40 percent within three months."  Original: "Helped manage social media." Rewritten: "Grew Instagram following from 5,000 to 25,000 in six months through a content series featuring customer stories."  Original: "Was responsible for the customer support team." Rewritten: "Managed a six person customer support team, reducing average response time from 8 hours to 90 minutes while maintaining a 92 percent satisfaction score."  Now rewrite:  Original: "Helped with the rollout of the new project management tool." Rewritten:
```

Template 6: Difficult Email Tone Adjustment

```
Rewrite each email to be more professional while maintaining the underlying message. Remove emotional reactivity. Maintain firmness on substance.  Examples: Original: "Honestly, this is the third time you have missed a deadline. I do not know what is going on but it has to stop." Rewritten: "I have noticed that this is the third missed deadline this quarter. I would like to understand what has been getting in the way so we can find a way to address it."  Original: "Your invoice is wrong AGAIN. Please fix it." Rewritten: "There appears to be an error on this invoice. I believe this is the second one this month with similar issues. Could you review and send a corrected version?"  Now rewrite:  Original:
```

```
"I am tired of the constant changes to the requirements. Make up your mind."
Rewritten:
```

Template 7: Technical Concept Explanation

```
Explain each technical concept to a curious non technical reader. Use a concrete
analogy and avoid jargon.  Examples:  Concept: API Explanation: An API is a
translator between two software systems. Think of a restaurant menu. The kitchen
knows how to make food, the customer knows what they want, but they speak
different languages. The menu lets them communicate in a structured way. APIs do
this for software.  Concept: Database index Explanation: A database index is
like the index at the back of a book. The book itself contains everything, but
the index tells you which pages mention what. Without an index, you would have
to flip through every page to find a specific topic. With one, you can jump
right there. Databases use indexes the same way to find information quickly.
Now explain:  Concept: Cache Explanation:
```

Template 8: Customer Story Extraction

```
Extract a customer success story from each interview transcript. Use this
structure: Challenge, Solution, Result.  Examples:  Transcript: "Yeah so we were
drowning in support tickets. Like 200 a day, three person team, things were just
slipping through. After we set up the auto categorization with their tool, we
cut the manual triage time in half. We are still getting 200 tickets but we
respond to the urgent ones in under an hour now, and our customer satisfaction
went up 12 points."  Story: Challenge: 200 daily support tickets overwhelming a
three person team and causing slipped responses. Solution: Implemented auto
categorization to reduce manual triage time. Result: Cut manual triage time in
half, urgent ticket response under one hour, customer satisfaction up 12 points.
Now extract:  Transcript: "Honestly it was a mess. We had four spreadsheets
tracking the same project across different teams, and they would always disagree
by Friday. Finally we just put everything in their tool. Now the four teams see
the same view, the disagreements stopped, and we shipped the product two weeks
ahead of schedule."  Story:
```

Template 9: User Story From Feature Description

```
Convert each feature description into a user story. Use the pattern: As a [user
type], I want [capability] so that [benefit].  Examples:  Feature: A search bar
at the top of the dashboard. User story: As a sales rep, I want to search across
all customer accounts so that I can find specific customers quickly without
scrolling through long lists.  Feature: Email notifications when a deal moves to
a new stage. User story: As a sales manager, I want to be notified when deals
```

```
advance so that I can stay aware of pipeline progress without having to check the dashboard manually.  Now convert:  Feature: Bulk export of all customer records to CSV. User story:
```

Template 10: Code Comment Generation

```
Add a one line comment above each function explaining what it does in plain English.  Examples:  Function: def calculate_discount(price, percentage): return price * (1 - percentage / 100)  With comment: # Returns the price after applying a percentage discount def calculate_discount(price, percentage): return price * (1 - percentage / 100)  Function: def get_active_users(users): return [u for u in users if u.last_login > thirty_days_ago()]  With comment: # Returns users who logged in within the past 30 days def get_active_users(users): return [u for u in users if u.last_login > thirty_days_ago()]  Now add comment: Function: def merge_sorted_lists(list1, list2):     result = []     i = j = 0 while i < len(list1) and j < len(list2):         if list1[i] <= list2[j]: result.append(list1[i])             i += 1         else: result.append(list2[j])             j += 1     result.extend(list1[i:]) result.extend(list2[j:])     return result
```

Template 11: Survey Question Refinement

```
Rewrite each survey question to be neutral and clear. Avoid leading language. Avoid double barreled questions.  Examples:  Original: "Don't you think our customer service is the best in the industry?" Rewritten: "How would you rate our customer service?"  Original: "Are you happy with our products and our prices?" Rewritten (split into two): "How satisfied are you with our products?" and "How satisfied are you with our prices?"  Now rewrite:  Original: "How much do you love our new dashboard design?" Rewritten:
```

Template 12: Announcement Tailoring

```
Tailor each announcement for a different audience while preserving the core message.  Examples:  Core message: We are shipping the new dashboard next Monday.  For engineering team: "Heads up: dashboard ship is next Monday. Final QA tomorrow, freeze begins Friday at 5 PM. Anything that needs to land must be in by then."  For customer success team: "The new dashboard ships Monday. Customer outreach kit is in the shared drive. Please review by Friday so you are ready for any inbound questions starting Monday morning."  For leadership: "Dashboard launches Monday on schedule. Customer success team is prepared with outreach materials. Tracking customer satisfaction in the first week as our primary success metric."  Now tailor for the design team:  Core message: We are shipping the new dashboard next Monday. For design team:
```

Building Your Few Shot Library

Save the few shot templates that work for tasks you do repeatedly. The investment of crafting the examples once pays back many times when the template handles dozens of subsequent inputs reliably. Few shot templates are some of the most leveraged assets in any prompt library.

Chapter 6: Step by Step Prompting

Some tasks are too complex for a single, monolithic prompt. They require thinking. They require working through multiple stages. They require, in some sense, the AI to reason rather than simply respond. The technique that addresses these tasks is called step by step prompting, sometimes also called chain of thought prompting in research literature.

The core idea is simple. Rather than asking for an answer in one shot, you guide the AI through a sequence of reasoning steps. Each step builds on the previous one. The final output is not just an answer. It is a thought process that culminates in an answer. This shift in approach unlocks tasks that would otherwise produce disappointing results.

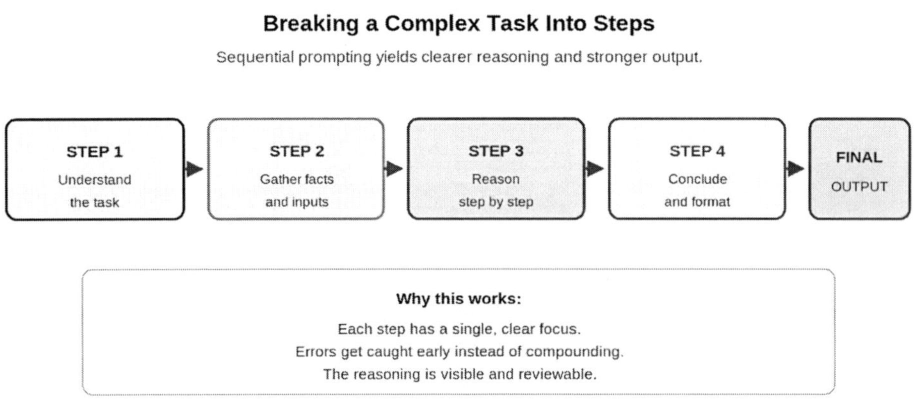

Figure 6.1: Breaking a complex task into clear sequential steps.

6.1 Breaking Tasks Into Steps

The first skill of step by step prompting is decomposition. You take a task that feels like one big problem and break it into smaller, more manageable problems. Each smaller problem is something the AI can solve well in a single step. The full task is then accomplished by stringing the steps together.

Consider a complex task like writing a strategic plan for a small business. As one big request, this would overwhelm even the best prompt. The AI would either produce something generic or skim several aspects superficially. But broken into steps, it becomes manageable. Step one, list the strengths and weaknesses of the business. Step two, identify the top three strategic opportunities. Step three, choose one opportunity and lay out a 90 day action plan. Step four, identify the resources and risks. Now each step has a clear focus, and the AI can do each step well.

How to Decompose a Task

Effective decomposition follows a few principles. The first principle is that each step should have a clear, single output. If you cannot describe what the output of a step looks like in one sentence, the step is probably too big. Break it further.

The second principle is that the output of one step should feed into the next. If step three depends on the result of step two, the chain has logic. If steps are independent, you might as well send them as separate prompts and combine them yourself.

The third principle is that the steps should match the natural reasoning a human expert would take. If you imagine a strategic consultant doing the same task, they would do it in stages, gathering information, analyzing options, evaluating risks, recommending a path. Your decomposition should mirror that natural flow. The AI works best when guided through a process that feels native to the kind of work being asked.

6.2 Guided Reasoning Prompts

Beyond simple decomposition, you can also use prompting techniques to encourage the AI to show its reasoning explicitly. The most famous is to add the phrase let us think step by step or let us reason this through carefully near the end of the prompt. This simple instruction often improves output dramatically, especially on tasks that involve logic, math, or multi factor analysis.

Why does such a simple addition help? Because asking the AI to think step by step changes the kind of output it produces. Instead of jumping to a conclusion, the AI lays out a reasoning chain first and then concludes. The reasoning chain forces the AI to confront the steps it would otherwise have skipped. Errors that would have lurked invisibly in a one shot answer become visible, and visible errors are correctable errors.

When to Ask for Visible Reasoning

Asking for visible reasoning works particularly well when the task involves any of the following: math problems with multiple operations, logic puzzles or constraint satisfaction, multi factor decisions where tradeoffs must be weighed, debugging or troubleshooting where root cause analysis matters, and complex classification where the rationale matters as much as the label.

It works less well for purely creative tasks or for tasks where the answer space is too narrow to need reasoning. Asking the AI to think step by step before producing a haiku is unnecessary and may even disrupt the flow of the creative output. Use guided reasoning where it helps, not as a universal addition to every prompt.

Examples of Guided Reasoning Prompts

```
A store sells apples for $2 each and oranges for $3 each. Maria buys 4 apples and some oranges. She spends $20 in total. How many oranges did she buy? Let us think step by step.

I have a project that needs to be done in three weeks. The team has 2 senior developers, 1 junior developer, and 1 designer. The work involves frontend, backend, and database changes. Help me allocate the work. Reason through the strengths and constraints of the team before recommending an allocation.
```

In each case, the prompt invites the AI to expose its reasoning before it commits to an answer. The output becomes both more accurate and more useful, because you can see the reasoning and validate it.

6.3 Sequential Instructions

Step by step prompts often use explicit sequential structure. The instruction itself is broken into numbered or labeled steps. The AI processes them in order. The output mirrors the structure. This is sometimes called sequential instruction prompting, and it is one of the most reliable patterns for complex work.

The structure of a sequential instruction prompt typically looks like this:

```
I want to plan a marketing campaign for a new product. Walk through the following steps in order and produce output for each.  Step 1: List three target customer segments most likely to want the product. Step 2: For each segment, suggest one channel where we can reach them effectively. Step 3: For each channel, draft a one sentence value proposition. Step 4: Recommend which segment we should prioritize first and explain why.  Produce the output in clearly labeled sections.
```

This structure is reliable because every step has a clear focus, every step builds on the previous, and the AI can produce a complete answer to the entire task without losing thread. The numbered steps also make the output easy to review and easy to revise. If step three feels weak, you can ask the AI to redo step three without redoing the entire task.

6.4 Improving Complex Outputs

Step by step prompting is particularly valuable when the output you need is complex. By complex we mean multi part, multi audience, or requiring multiple kinds of reasoning. Examples include strategic plans, technical proposals, multi section reports, code with explanations, lesson plans, or any deliverable that pulls together several distinct kinds of work.

Without step by step structure, complex outputs tend to be uneven. The AI may do one part well and the others sketchily. The first part of a long output may be polished and the last part rushed. The transitions between parts may feel jarring or contradictory. Step by step structure prevents this by giving each part its own moment of focused attention.

The Compounding Quality Effect

There is a useful concept worth highlighting. We can call it the compounding quality effect. When the AI produces output one step at a time, with each step focused on a single thing, the quality of each step is higher than it would be if all steps were produced in one shot. And because each step builds on the prior one, the high quality of step one improves step two, the high quality of step two improves step three, and so on. The improvements compound.

This is why step by step prompting often produces output that feels qualitatively better than what a one shot prompt would produce, even when the prompts cover the same task. The structure is not just organizational. It is generative.

6.5 Avoiding Confusion in Multi Step Prompts

Multi step prompts are powerful, but they can also fail in characteristic ways. Knowing the failure modes helps you design prompts that avoid them.

Failure Mode One: Too Many Steps

If a prompt has eight, ten, or more steps, the AI may begin to lose coherence. Earlier steps fade from attention. Later steps get rushed. The output for any given step may be shallower than it would be if the prompt were broken into multiple separate prompts. The threshold varies, but as a guideline, three to five steps per prompt is comfortable. Six or seven works for some tasks. Beyond that, consider splitting the prompt.

Failure Mode Two: Steps That Overlap

If two steps cover similar ground, the AI may produce redundant output, or it may merge the two steps into one. Each step should have a distinct focus that the others do not address. If you find two steps overlapping, merge them into one or refine each to handle a non overlapping aspect.

Failure Mode Three: Steps That Are Disconnected

If the steps do not build on each other, the prompt is really just several independent prompts in a trench coat. You may as well send them separately. Strong multi step prompts have an internal logic where each step uses what came before. If you cannot articulate that logic, reconsider whether the task really needs to be one prompt.

Failure Mode Four: Vague Steps

Each step needs a concrete output. Steps like consider the implications or think about the audience are too vague. The AI does not know what shape the output of that step should take. Replace vague steps with concrete ones, like list the three most important implications and rank them by impact.

> **Multi Step Prompt Checklist**
>
> Three to five steps. Each with a concrete output. Each connected to the next. Each focused on a distinct aspect. Together forming a logical flow that mirrors how an expert would approach the task. When all five qualities are present, multi step prompts produce excellent results.

6.6 Chapter Recap

This chapter introduced step by step prompting as a technique for handling complex tasks.

- Decompose complex tasks into smaller, more manageable sub problems, each with a clear single output.
- Encourage visible reasoning by asking the AI to think step by step on tasks that involve logic, math, or multi factor analysis.
- Use sequential instruction prompts with numbered or labeled steps for complex deliverables.
- Step by step structure produces a compounding quality effect, where each step builds on the prior to lift overall output quality.
- Avoid common failure modes by limiting steps, ensuring each is distinct, connecting them logically, and giving each a concrete output.

Practice Exercise

The difference between a one shot prompt and a decomposed multi step prompt becomes obvious when you run them on the same task.

1. Pick a complex task you would normally ask an AI to handle in one shot. A research summary, a strategic analysis, or a technical explanation works well.
2. First, run the task as a single one shot prompt and save the output.
3. Decompose the same task into three to five sequential steps. Each step should have a clear, concrete output.
4. Write the multi step prompt and run it. Save the output.

5. Compare both outputs side by side. Look for depth of reasoning, completeness, and how naturally the second version flows.

The decomposed version usually produces output that feels like it was written by someone who took their time, because in a sense it was.

6.7 The Cognitive Science Behind Step by Step Prompting

Section 6.1 covered task decomposition. This expansion looks at why step by step prompting works so well from a cognitive perspective, drawing on insights from how humans solve complex problems.

Working Memory and Cognitive Load

Human problem solving research has long recognized that working memory is limited. We can only hold a small number of distinct items in active attention at once. When a problem demands more, our performance degrades. We make errors. We skip steps. We arrive at incorrect answers because we could not hold all the relevant information at once. The fix that humans discovered, long ago, is to externalize the work. Write things down. Use diagrams. Break the problem into stages. Each stage has a manageable load.

AI systems share an analog of this pattern. While they do not have working memory in the human sense, they have a kind of attention budget that gets stretched across long, complex prompts. When a single prompt asks for too much at once, the AI may produce output that misses connections, skips reasoning, or arrives at conclusions that do not follow from the inputs. Step by step prompting addresses this by giving the AI smaller, more focused units of work to do.

Why Visible Reasoning Helps

Asking the AI to reason out loud, step by step, also has a cognitive parallel in human practice. Researchers have found that humans solve problems better when they verbalize their reasoning, partly because the act of articulation forces them to be precise. Vague mental shortcuts that would otherwise slide by become visible and correctable when forced into words.

AI systems show a similar pattern. When asked to produce a final answer directly, they may take cognitive shortcuts that are hard to spot. When asked to show their reasoning first, they expose the steps. Errors in the steps become visible. The final answer is more likely to be correct because the reasoning is visible. This is why phrases like let us think step by step often improve output quality measurably.

6.8 Decomposition Patterns

Section 6.1 introduced decomposition principles. This expansion looks at recurring patterns of decomposition that work for different kinds of complex tasks. Each pattern is a starting point you can adapt.

The Investigate Then Recommend Pattern

Many decision support tasks decompose naturally into investigation followed by recommendation. Step one gathers facts. Step two analyzes them. Step three recommends. This pattern resists the temptation to jump to a recommendation without grounding it in analysis.

```
Three steps:  1. Investigate. Read the situation below and list the most
relevant facts. 2. Analyze. Identify the key trade offs implied by those facts.
3. Recommend. Propose a single course of action with justification tied to the
trade offs.
```

The Compare Then Choose Pattern

Decision tasks involving multiple options decompose into comparison followed by selection. Step one establishes the criteria. Step two compares the options against the criteria. Step three picks the best option.

```
Three steps:  1. List the four most important criteria for evaluating these
options, given the use case described above. 2. Compare each option against each
criterion in a table. 3. Recommend the best option, with a one paragraph
justification anchored in the comparison.
```

The Diverge Then Converge Pattern

Creative tasks often benefit from diverging widely before converging on a single direction. Step one generates many options. Step two evaluates them. Step three selects and develops.

```
Three steps:  1. Generate ten possible angles for this article. 2. Evaluate each
angle against these criteria: novelty, relevance, and feasibility. 3. Pick the
strongest angle and write a 100 word article outline based on it.
```

The Draft Then Critique Pattern

Writing tasks improve when the AI critiques its own draft before producing the final version. Step one drafts. Step two critiques. Step three rewrites.

```
Three steps:  1. Draft a 200 word version of the announcement. 2. Critique the
draft against these criteria: clarity, brevity, warmth, and accuracy. 3. Rewrite
the announcement to address the critique. Show only the final version.
```

The Extract Then Transform Pattern

Data processing tasks decompose into extraction followed by transformation. Step one pulls the relevant data from the source. Step two restructures it. Step three formats the result.

```
Three steps:  1. Extract all dates, names, and decisions from the meeting
transcript. 2. Group them into a structured timeline. 3. Format the timeline as
a markdown table with columns Date, Decision, Owner.
```

The Layered Edit Pattern

Editing tasks improve when broken into layers, each focused on a different dimension. Step one fixes structure. Step two fixes clarity. Step three polishes voice.

```
Three steps:  1. Identify any structural problems in the article. Suggest a
restructured outline. 2. Apply the restructure and rewrite the article. Identify
any clarity problems in the new version. Fix them. 3. Polish the voice for
warmth and rhythm. Show the final version.
```

6.9 Guided Reasoning: Beyond Let Us Think Step by Step

Section 6.2 introduced guided reasoning. This expansion explores variations of the technique and when each works best.

The Show Your Reasoning Variant

Adding show your reasoning before answering invites the AI to expose its thinking. This variant works particularly well for math problems and constraint satisfaction tasks where the reasoning is the whole point.

```
A train leaves Chicago at 9 AM going east at 60 miles per hour. Another train
leaves Detroit at 11 AM going west at 50 miles per hour. The cities are 280
miles apart. At what time will they meet? Show your reasoning before giving the
final answer.
```

The Justify Each Step Variant

Asking the AI to justify each step of its reasoning surfaces assumptions that would otherwise be hidden. This variant works well for tasks where the reasoning depends on premises that should be checked.

```
Should this customer churn risk model use last 7 days of usage or last 30 days?
Walk through the reasoning, justifying each step, before giving a
recommendation.
```

The Consider Alternatives Variant

Asking the AI to consider alternatives before recommending forces it to weigh options rather than commit prematurely. This variant works well for decision tasks with multiple plausible answers.

```
Recommend a database for this application. Before giving your recommendation,
briefly consider three alternatives and explain why your chosen one fits best
given the constraints described above.
```

The Identify Uncertainty Variant

Asking the AI to flag what it is uncertain about reduces hallucination by inviting honest gaps. This variant works well when accuracy matters and the AI's confident tone could mislead.

```
Analyze the financial summary below. Before giving your conclusions, identify
any numbers or claims you are uncertain about, and explain the source of the
uncertainty. Then give the analysis.
```

6.10 Sequential Instructions: Three Detailed Examples

Section 6.3 introduced sequential instructions. Below are three detailed examples for different kinds of work.

Example 1: Strategic Planning

```
I want to plan a marketing strategy for our new product. Walk through the
following steps in order, producing labeled output for each.  Step 1: List three
target customer segments most likely to want this product. Step 2: For each
segment, suggest one channel where we can reach them effectively given a $2,000
monthly budget. Step 3: For each channel, draft a one sentence value
proposition. Step 4: Recommend which segment we should prioritize first, and
explain why in two sentences.  Product: A subscription service that delivers
monthly themed boxes of high quality stationery and writing tools to
professionals who want to write more by hand.
```

Example 2: Code Refactoring

```
I have a Python function that has grown messy over time. Walk through the
following steps in order.  Step 1: Read the function below and identify three
specific issues that hurt readability or maintainability. Step 2: For each
issue, propose a specific refactor. Step 3: Apply all three refactors and
produce a clean version of the function. Step 4: Add a docstring and inline
comments where they would help.  [Code] ...
```

Example 3: Lesson Plan Design

```
Help me design a 45 minute lesson on photosynthesis for ninth grade biology.
Walk through the following steps in order.  Step 1: Identify the three most
important learning objectives for this topic at this grade level. Step 2: For
each objective, propose one short activity that helps students achieve it. Step
3: Sketch a 45 minute lesson plan timeline that includes warm up, the three
activities, and a closing reflection. Step 4: Suggest one assessment question
for each objective.
```

6.11 Avoiding Step by Step Failure Modes

Section 6.5 covered failure modes. This expansion adds depth to each, with diagnostic questions and concrete repairs.

Failure Mode: Steps That Look Good but Do Not Build

Sometimes a multi step prompt has well written steps that do not actually depend on each other. Step one produces facts. Step two produces analysis. Step three produces recommendations. Each is a complete thought. But the recommendations do not actually use the analysis, and the analysis does not actually use the facts. The steps are independent monoliths.

The diagnosis is to ask, does step three's output meaningfully change if step two changes? If no, the chain is broken. The repair is to phrase later steps so they explicitly build on earlier output. Replace produce recommendations with based on the analysis above, produce recommendations that address the issues identified.

Failure Mode: Steps That Are Internally Inconsistent

Sometimes the AI produces output for one step that contradicts what it produced earlier. Step two might claim a customer segment is the most valuable, but step four recommends a different segment. The reasoning between them was lost.

The repair is to ask the AI to reference its own earlier output explicitly. Add phrases like building on the segments identified in step one or referring back to the trade offs from step two. Explicit references force the AI to maintain coherence across the chain.

Failure Mode: Steps That Run Together

Sometimes the AI's output blurs the steps, producing one continuous response rather than clearly labeled stages. The structure you wanted is invisible in the final output.

The repair is to make the labels explicit and ask the AI to use them. Phrases like start each step with a bold heading like Step 1, Step 2, and so on, or produce output in clearly labeled sections force the structure to appear.

> **Step by Step Health Check**
>
> Healthy multi step prompts have steps that each have a clear focused output, build on each other meaningfully, are clearly labeled in the response, and produce coherent output that hangs together. If any of these is missing, the chain is weaker than it could be.

6.12 When Not to Use Step by Step Prompting

Step by step prompting is powerful, but it is not always the right tool. Several situations call for simpler approaches.

- Quick factual lookups. Asking what is the capital of France in three steps is silly. The direct prompt is right.
- Single sentence transformations. Translate this phrase to French does not need decomposition.
- Pure creativity. Step by step structure can drain spontaneity from poems, jokes, or short fiction. The structure forces a kind of analytic mode that may not serve creative tasks.
- When you need speed. Multi step prompts produce longer responses that take more time. For tasks where speed matters more than depth, simpler prompts win.
- When the task is genuinely simple. If a task is one cognitive step, splitting it into three is artificial and may produce padded output.

The skill is matching the prompt complexity to the task complexity. Simple tasks deserve simple prompts. Complex tasks deserve thoughtful decomposition. The middle ground, moderately complex tasks, can usually go either way, with judgment determining which is more efficient.

6.13 Multi Step Prompts in Detail: Eight Worked Patterns

Section 6.10 introduced sequential instructions. Below are eight more multi step patterns, each with a worked example for a different domain. Read these as reference patterns you can adapt. The structure is what matters, not the specific topic of each example.

Pattern: Investigate Then Synthesize

```
Three steps:  1. Read the customer support tickets below and identify recurring
complaint themes. 2. For each theme, count how many tickets mention it and
provide three representative quotes. 3. Synthesize a one paragraph summary of
what the data tells us about customer experience right now.  [Tickets]
```

Pattern: Diagnose Then Prescribe

```
Three steps:  1. Read the website analytics below. Identify the three most concerning trends. 2. For each trend, hypothesize the most likely cause based on the data. 3. For each cause, recommend one experiment we could run to confirm or refute it.  [Analytics]
```

Pattern: Compare Then Recommend

```
Three steps:  1. List the four most important criteria for choosing among these vendors, given that we are a 50 person company prioritizing reliability and ease of use. 2. Score each vendor against each criterion on a scale of 1 to 5. 3. Recommend a vendor with a one paragraph rationale anchored in the scores. [Vendor information]
```

Pattern: Translate Then Verify

```
Three steps:  1. Translate the document below from English to French. 2. Review your translation. Identify any phrases where the meaning may have shifted or where culture specific references could confuse a French reader. 3. Provide a revised translation that addresses any issues you identified.  [Document]
```

Pattern: Outline Then Develop

```
Three steps:  1. Produce a detailed outline for an article about climate adaptation in coastal cities. The outline should have an introduction, four main sections, and a conclusion. Each section should have three bullet points indicating its main ideas. 2. Develop the introduction (about 200 words). 3. Develop the first main section (about 400 words).
```

Pattern: Question Generation Then Answer

```
Three steps:  1. Read the policy document below. Generate the ten most important questions a stakeholder would want answered after reading it. 2. For each question, indicate whether it is fully answered in the document, partially answered, or not addressed. 3. For the not addressed questions, suggest what additional information would be needed to answer them.
```

Pattern: Risk Identification Then Mitigation

```
Three steps:  1. Read the project plan below. Identify the five most significant risks that could cause the project to fail or significantly delay. 2. For each risk, estimate the likelihood (high, medium, low) and the impact (high, medium, low). 3. For the high likelihood, high impact risks, propose one concrete mitigation each.
```

Pattern: Argument Generation Then Counter Argument

```
Three steps:  1. Make the strongest case in favor of [proposal], using three arguments grounded in evidence from the source material below. 2. For each argument, identify the strongest counter argument a thoughtful skeptic would raise. 3. Propose one synthesis position that acknowledges the strongest counter arguments while still supporting the original proposal.
```

Each of these patterns produces output that is more rigorous than a single direct prompt could. The structure forces the AI to do work in multiple stages rather than collapsing complexity into a single response. The investment in structure pays back in output quality.

6.14 Step by Step Prompting for Specific Domains

The general patterns above adapt to specific domains. Here are domain specific applications of step by step prompting that produce reliably useful output.

Step by Step for Code Refactoring

```
Four steps:  1. Read the function below. Identify three issues affecting readability, robustness, or correctness. 2. For each issue, propose a specific fix. 3. Apply all three fixes and produce the refactored function. 4. Add a docstring summarizing the function's purpose and arguments.
```

Step by Step for User Research

```
Three steps:  1. Read the interview transcripts below. Identify three behavioral patterns shared across multiple interviewees. 2. For each pattern, articulate the underlying user goal it suggests. 3. For each goal, propose one specific feature that would help users achieve it.
```

Step by Step for Strategic Planning

```
Four steps:  1. Identify three strategic priorities for our company over the next year, based on the market analysis below. 2. For each priority, define what success would look like at the end of the year. 3. For each priority, identify the most significant obstacle and a specific way to address it. 4. Synthesize into a one page strategy memo with sections Priorities, Success Metrics, and Critical Moves.
```

Step by Step for Hiring

```
Three steps:  1. Based on the role description below, identify five capabilities a strong candidate must demonstrate. 2. For each capability, propose two
```

```
interview questions that would surface it. 3. For each question, indicate what a strong answer would include and what a weak answer would look like.
```

Step by Step for Editorial Work

```
Three steps:  1. Read the draft below. Identify the three most significant structural issues, where structure means how the piece is organized rather than how individual sentences are written. 2. Propose a revised outline that addresses the structural issues while preserving the author's main argument and evidence. 3. Identify the three most significant prose issues. Propose specific edits without rewriting the whole piece.
```

Domain Adaptation

The general patterns of step by step prompting apply across domains. The skill is recognizing the kind of multi stage work each domain requires and adapting the pattern accordingly. Build domain specific templates as you encounter recurring needs in your work.

Chapter 7: Iterative Prompting

In a perfect world, every prompt would produce exactly the right output on the first try. In practice, many prompts produce something close to right but not quite. The output is too long. Or too short. Or covers the right ground but in the wrong tone. Or includes a section you did not want, or missed one you did. The skill of moving from this near miss to a perfect output is iterative prompting, the deliberate practice of refining a prompt over multiple rounds.

Iterative prompting is one of the most underrated skills in working with AI. Beginners often stop after the first attempt. They look at a near miss and conclude that the AI is not capable of the task. Skilled prompt writers see a near miss as a starting point. They iterate, refine, and reshape until the output is what they want. This chapter is about that practice.

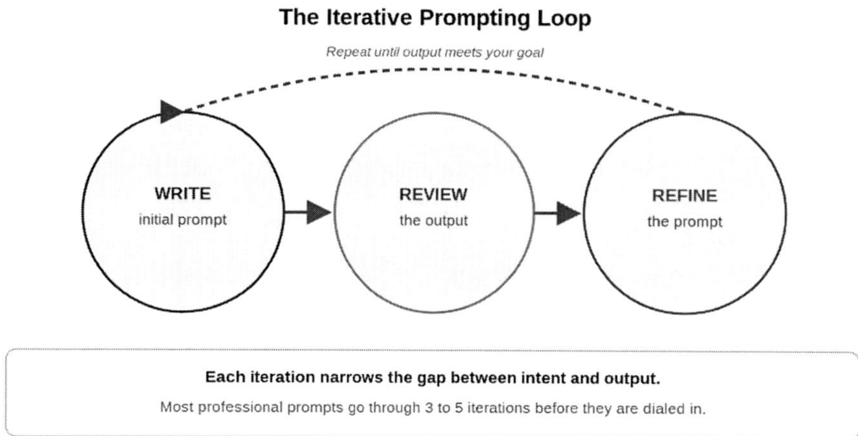

Figure 7.1: The iterative prompting loop, where each round narrows the gap between intent and output.

7.1 Refining Prompts Based on Output

Iteration starts with a careful read of what the AI produced. Before changing the prompt, study the output. What is right? What is wrong? What is missing? What is extra? The answers to these questions guide the next iteration. Without this analysis, you risk changing the wrong thing and making the prompt worse.

Diagnosing the Output

There is a useful framework for diagnosing AI output. Compare what you got to what you wanted along four dimensions.

Dimension	Question to Ask	If Off, Likely Cause
Substance	Did the AI cover the right content?	Instruction was vague or missing key elements.
Structure	Is the output organized the way you want?	Output expectation was not specified clearly.
Style	Does the tone, voice, or vocabulary fit?	Tonal constraints were missing or unclear.
Scale	Is the length right? Too long? Too short?	Length constraints were absent or imprecise.

Once you have diagnosed which dimensions are off, you know where to focus your iteration. If substance is off, refine the instruction or add context. If structure is off, specify the output format more clearly. If style is off, add tonal constraints. If scale is off, add length constraints. Targeted refinement is more efficient than broad rewriting.

7.2 Asking Follow Up Prompts

One form of iteration does not require rewriting the original prompt at all. You can simply send a follow up prompt that builds on what the AI already produced. This works because most AI chat interfaces preserve the conversation context, allowing the AI to refer back to its prior outputs.

Follow up prompts can take many forms. They can ask for revisions, like make this shorter or rewrite this in a more formal tone. They can ask for additions, like add a paragraph about pricing. They can ask for variations, like give me three more options. They can ask for explanations, like why did you recommend that approach. Each follow up shapes the conversation and brings the output closer to your goal.

Effective Follow Up Patterns

Some follow up patterns are particularly effective. The narrowing follow up asks the AI to focus on a specific part of its prior output, like expand the section on risks into more detail. The expanding follow up asks the AI to broaden, like give me three more options like the second one you suggested. The shifting follow up asks the AI to change tone or angle, like rewrite this for a more skeptical audience. The simplifying follow up asks the AI to reduce or compress, like give me a one paragraph version of this for an executive summary.

Each pattern serves a different purpose, and combining them across multiple turns of conversation often produces output that no single prompt could have produced. The AI's first attempt becomes raw material for refinement. The conversation becomes the medium of creation.

7.3 Narrowing Down Responses

Sometimes the AI's first response is too broad. It covers many aspects of a topic when you wanted depth on one. It offers many options when you wanted a strong recommendation. The technique for handling this is narrowing, where each follow up reduces the scope of the response until it focuses on exactly what you need.

A narrowing sequence might look like this. First prompt, give me ten ideas for blog post topics about productivity. The AI returns ten ideas. Second prompt, of those ten, which three would resonate most with first time managers, and why. The AI narrows to three with rationale. Third prompt, expand idea two into a 200 word outline with three subsections. The AI expands one of the three into a working outline. Through this sequence, you have moved from broad exploration to a specific deliverable in three short prompts, none of which would have produced the deliverable on their own.

7.4 Expanding or Simplifying Outputs

The opposite of narrowing is expanding, where each follow up adds breadth, depth, or detail. Expanding works well when the AI's first response is correct but too thin. You take the strong skeleton and ask the AI to flesh it out part by part.

Simplification is also a common iterative move. The first response may be technically accurate but too dense. You ask the AI to simplify, perhaps for a different audience, perhaps just for readability. The second response is more accessible. If it loses too much, you ask for a balance, the same simplicity but with one specific concept restored in detail. Through these moves, you converge on the right level of complexity for your audience.

Calibrating Length and Depth

Iterative calibration of length and depth is one of the most common forms of refinement. The AI rarely produces output of exactly the length and depth you want on the first try. But it responds reliably to instructions like make this half as long, expand this by twice the length, or add a layer of detail to each section. By moving in either direction across iterations, you can dial in to your target with surprising precision.

A useful technique is to ask for output that is too long or too short on purpose. If you want 200 words and the AI produces 300, you might iterate down to 200 directly. But if you produce 500 first, you can then ask for 200, and the AI will preserve the most important parts and drop the less important ones. Sometimes producing a long version first and compressing later produces better output than asking for the right length up front.

7.5 Prompt Chaining Basics

Prompt chaining is a more structured form of iteration. Instead of having a free flowing conversation, you design a deliberate sequence of prompts where the output of each prompt becomes the input to the next. The chain produces a final result through a series of intermediate steps that each produce something useful.

Prompt chains differ from multi step prompts in an important way. In a multi step prompt, all the steps are described in a single prompt and the AI processes them together. In a prompt chain, each step is its own prompt, sent separately, and you control what passes from one to the next. This gives you more control. You can review and adjust each intermediate output before moving to the next step.

A Simple Chain Example

Consider a writing project with four stages: research, outline, draft, and edit.

1. Prompt 1: Research. Generate a list of the ten most important facts and arguments to consider when writing about the topic.
2. Prompt 2: Outline. Based on those facts and arguments, propose a three section outline for an article.
3. Prompt 3: Draft. Write a 600 word article following the outline above.
4. Prompt 4: Edit. Edit the draft below for clarity, rhythm, and concision. Preserve the structure but tighten the language.

Each prompt is its own focused task. Each output feeds into the next. You can review the research before approving it for the outline. You can adjust the outline before approving it for the draft. You can rewrite parts of the draft before sending it to the edit step. The chain gives you control points where you can shape the final result.

When to Use a Chain Versus a Single Prompt

Use a single prompt when the task is small, when you trust the AI to handle the steps internally, and when speed matters. Use a chain when the task is larger, when each stage benefits from review, when you want to combine outputs from multiple sources, or when you need to inject your own judgment between stages. Chains are slower but produce more reliable, higher quality output for non trivial work.

Iterative Mindset

The best AI users do not try to write the perfect prompt on the first try. They write a reasonable prompt, look at the output, identify what is off, and iterate. Iteration is not a sign of failure. It is the craft. The fewer prompts you need to reach your target, the more efficient your iteration. But the iteration itself is the work.

7.6 Chapter Recap

This chapter covered iterative prompting and its variants.

- Diagnose the output along four dimensions before iterating: substance, structure, style, and scale.
- Use targeted follow up prompts to refine, narrow, expand, or shift the output without rewriting the original prompt.
- Calibrate length and depth iteratively. Sometimes producing too much and trimming back produces better output than aiming for exact length on the first try.
- Prompt chains are deliberate sequences where each prompt's output feeds the next. They give you control points and produce reliable results on complex work.
- Iteration is the craft, not a sign of failure. Skilled prompt writers reach their target through several rounds, each one improving on the last.

Practice Exercise

This exercise builds your fluency with prompt chains by running a complete writing task through one.

1. Pick a writing task you have been putting off. An article, a memo, or a longer post all work.
2. Send Prompt 1: research. Ask the AI to gather facts and key arguments on the topic.
3. Send Prompt 2: outline. Based on the research output, ask for a three section outline.
4. Send Prompt 3: draft. Ask for a full draft following the outline.
5. Send Prompt 4: edit. Ask the AI to tighten the draft for clarity, rhythm, and concision.
6. At each step, review and adjust the output before passing it to the next stage. The review points are where the chain delivers most of its value.
7. Compare the final result to what you would have produced asking for the article in a single one shot prompt.

The chain produces a noticeably more thoughtful and polished result for almost any non trivial topic, because each stage gets the attention it deserves.

7.7 The Diagnostic Vocabulary

Section 7.1 introduced diagnosing output along four dimensions. This expansion provides a richer diagnostic vocabulary for naming what is wrong with an AI output, which makes iteration faster and more targeted.

Substance Issues

Symptom	Likely Cause	Repair
Misses the question entirely	Instruction was vague or task was misframed	Sharpen the instruction with a clear verb
Covers the wrong angle	Audience or purpose was missing	Add audience and intent
Is generically true but uninformative	No specific context to ground in	Provide source material or detailed context
Hedges too much	Lack of clear stance requested	Explicitly ask for a recommendation
Includes invented facts	AI filled gaps it could not actually fill	Bound to source material; ask to flag uncertainty

Structure Issues

Symptom	Likely Cause	Repair
Wrong format	No format specified	Specify the format explicitly
Inconsistent format across items	No example or template	Provide a skeleton or use few shot
Sections do not balance	No length guidance per section	Specify approximate length per section

Symptom	Likely Cause	Repair
Missing sections you wanted	Output expectation incomplete	List the required sections explicitly
Sections in wrong order	No order indicated	Specify the order of sections

Style Issues

Symptom	Likely Cause	Repair
Tone is too formal	Default register kicked in	Specify casual or warm tone
Tone is too informal	No formality cue	Specify professional tone
Voice does not match brand	No voice example provided	Provide a sample of the desired voice
Vocabulary too technical	Audience not specified	Specify a non technical audience
Vocabulary too simple	Audience not specified	Specify expert audience

Scale Issues

Symptom	Likely Cause	Repair
Way too long	No length limit	Specify a maximum length
Way too short	Length limit too tight or no minimum	Specify a minimum or expected length
Sections imbalanced in length	No section sizing guidance	Specify size per section
Bullets too verbose	No bullet length guidance	Specify one sentence per bullet
Bullets too terse	Bullets defaulted to phrases	Specify complete sentences per bullet

Having a precise vocabulary for what is wrong with output is a quiet superpower. It means each iteration is targeted. You are not vaguely rewriting. You are making a specific change to address a specific symptom. The result is fewer iterations to reach your target.

7.8 Follow Up Prompt Patterns

Section 7.2 introduced follow up prompts. This expansion provides a deeper catalog of follow up patterns and the situations they handle.

The Compression Follow Up

```
That was helpful but too long. Give me the same content in 100 words or fewer,
preserving the most important points.
```

Compression follow ups distill the AI's first response into a tighter version. Useful when the first attempt was thorough but exceeded what fits your purpose.

The Expansion Follow Up

```
Expand on the third point. Give me a paragraph that explains the underlying
reasoning and includes one concrete example.
```

Expansion follow ups develop a piece of the response. Useful when the first attempt was a good outline but a section deserves depth.

The Variation Follow Up

```
Give me three more options like the second one. I liked its tone but want more
candidates in that style.
```

Variation follow ups produce more candidates of a particular type. Useful when the first response had one option you liked and you want to see others in the same vein.

The Pivot Follow Up

```
Now redo this for a different audience. Same content, but written for executives
who want the bottom line first.
```

Pivot follow ups shift audience, tone, or angle while keeping the substance. Useful when the same content needs to reach multiple groups.

The Critique Follow Up

```
Critique what you just wrote. What are its three biggest weaknesses?
```

Critique follow ups invite the AI to evaluate its own output. Useful as a midpoint between draft and revision, since the AI's critique reveals what to address.

The Revision Follow Up

```
Take your previous response and rewrite it to fix the three weaknesses you just identified.
```

Revision follow ups apply the critique. Combined with the critique follow up, this two step pattern often produces output dramatically better than the first attempt.

The Justification Follow Up

```
Why did you choose option B over option A? Walk me through the reasoning.
```

Justification follow ups expose the reasoning behind a recommendation. Useful when you need to validate the AI's logic before relying on it.

The Edge Case Follow Up

```
How would your recommendation change if the budget were half as large?
```

Edge case follow ups stress test the response by changing one variable. Useful for evaluating robustness.

7.9 The Skilled Iterator's Mindset

Beyond techniques, iterative prompting is a mindset. The skilled iterator approaches AI work with a particular set of attitudes that make their iteration efficient.

Curiosity Over Frustration

When a response is not what you wanted, the skilled iterator gets curious rather than frustrated. What about this output is off? Why might the AI have produced this? What was missing in my prompt? The curious frame makes diagnosis easier and faster than the frustrated frame, which tends to provoke vague rewrites that may not address the actual issue.

Specificity Over Vagueness

When refining, the skilled iterator makes specific changes rather than broad rewrites. They add a single constraint, change a single phrase, or include a single example. The targeted change isolates which intervention helps. Broad rewrites obscure cause and effect.

Patience Over Haste

The skilled iterator is willing to spend three or four rounds on an important prompt before declaring it done. They know that the marginal time spent on iteration usually pays back in output quality. Hasty iterators stop too early and accept worse results.

Documentation Over Memory

The skilled iterator notes what worked. When they find a prompt that produces excellent output, they save it. When they find a useful follow up pattern, they remember it for next time. Their iteration knowledge accumulates across sessions, building a personal craft library.

7.10 Prompt Chaining: Advanced Patterns

Section 7.5 introduced prompt chaining. This expansion looks at advanced chaining patterns that handle complex workflows.

The Linear Chain

The simplest chain runs sequentially: A produces B, B produces C, C produces D. Each prompt's output becomes the next prompt's input. Linear chains work for tasks with a clear sequential structure, like research, outline, draft, edit.

The Branching Chain

More complex chains have branches. Prompt A produces B. From B, two parallel prompts produce C1 and C2. The user chooses one, and the chain continues. Branching chains handle tasks where intermediate decisions affect the path forward.

The Iterative Chain

Iterative chains include feedback loops. Prompt A produces draft. Prompt B critiques the draft. Prompt C revises based on the critique. The cycle may repeat until the output is satisfactory. Iterative chains produce especially polished output for high stakes work.

The Aggregation Chain

Aggregation chains pull multiple parallel outputs together. Prompts A1, A2, A3 each handle a different aspect of a problem. Prompt B synthesizes their outputs into a unified result. Aggregation chains work for multi faceted analysis where each facet deserves its own focused attention.

Chaining Trade Offs

Chains produce higher quality output than single prompts for complex work. They also take longer, since each prompt is its own round trip. They are more expensive in token usage. They require you to maintain state between prompts. The trade off is quality and control versus speed and simplicity.

For routine work, single prompts win. For important deliverables, chains often produce dramatically better results. The skill is matching the technique to the stakes. Reserve chains for the work where the extra effort pays off.

7.11 Real World Iteration Walkthrough

Below is a complete walkthrough of iterative prompting on a real task. The task is writing an executive summary of a product launch retrospective for an internal email.

Iteration 1: First Attempt

```
Write an executive summary of our product launch retrospective for an email to
leadership.
```

The output is competent but generic. It uses standard executive summary phrasing, hits five hundred words, and reads like every other executive summary the AI has ever produced. It is not bad, but it does not feel like ours.

Iteration 2: Add Context

```
Write an executive summary of our product launch retrospective for an email to
leadership. The launch was for our new mobile app. Adoption is below target, but
engagement among adopters is exceptionally high. Leadership cares most about the
bottom line and tends to skim. Tone should be honest about the adoption gap
without being defeatist.
```

The output is more focused. It addresses the specific situation, mentions the engagement strength alongside the adoption gap, and adopts a more honest tone. Still too long, around four hundred words.

Iteration 3: Tighten Length

```
Same task, but in 200 words or fewer. Open with the bottom line. Use three short
paragraphs.
```

Now we get a tight 195 word summary, opens with the bottom line, three paragraphs. Format is right. But the second paragraph still feels generic.

Iteration 4: Address the Specific Weakness

```
That second paragraph reads as if it could describe any product. Replace it with
two specific findings from the retrospective: that engagement among adopters is
double the industry average, and that adoption is being limited by an onboarding
flow that drops 40 percent of users on the first screen.
```

Now the second paragraph is specific and powerful. The summary as a whole is sharp.

Iteration 5: Final Polish

```
Last pass. Soften the opening sentence so it does not sound alarmist. Keep
everything else.
```

After this pass, the summary is exactly right. Five iterations, each focused on a specific issue, took about ten minutes. The result is dramatically better than what any single prompt could have produced.

> **The Pattern of Iteration**
>
> Five iterations is typical for important work. The first establishes a baseline. The next two or three address the biggest issues. The final one or two polish details. Skilled iterators expect this rhythm and budget time for it. Beginners give up after iteration one and miss the eighty percent improvement that lies in the next four.

7.12 An Extended Walkthrough of Iterative Prompting

Section 7.11 walked through a brief iteration. Below is a longer walkthrough showing iterative prompting on a more complex task: developing a strategic memo for a leadership team. The walkthrough has eight rounds. Each round shows what the user asked, what the output produced, and what the user noticed.

Round 1: Initial Request

User: Write a strategic memo about our customer churn problem for the leadership team.

AI output: A 600 word memo covering churn definitions, common causes, and generic recommendations. Reads like a business school case study.

User notices: The memo is too generic. It does not reference any specifics about our company. It treats churn as an abstract problem rather than our problem.

Round 2: Add Context

User: Add context. We are a B2B SaaS company with 1,200 customers. Our annual churn rate is 18 percent, up from 12 percent two years ago. The biggest segment of churn is small customers (under 10 employees) who churn within the first six months. The leadership team has heard several explanations for this trend already and is skeptical of more theories without action.

AI output: A 550 word memo grounded in our specific situation. Discusses small customer churn pattern. Suggests onboarding improvements.

User notices: The memo is more specific but the recommendations are still generic onboarding suggestions. They do not feel like they would convince leadership to act.

Round 3: Sharpen Recommendations

User: The recommendations are too generic. Leadership wants three specific, testable bets we could make in the next quarter, each with an estimated impact and an estimated cost. Replace the recommendations section accordingly.

AI output: Three specific recommendations with estimated impact ranges and cost ranges. Onboarding redesign, dedicated small customer success role, in product retention prompts.

User notices: Better. But the cost estimates feel made up. The AI does not know our actual costs.

Round 4: Frame Estimates Honestly

User: For the cost and impact estimates, frame them as ranges with the assumptions underlying each estimate. Do not commit to specific numbers we cannot defend.

AI output: Estimates revised to ranges with explicit assumptions. The memo now reads as honest analysis rather than false precision.

User notices: Good. Now the structure feels off. The memo opens with definitions and ends with recommendations. Leadership wants the bottom line first.

Round 5: Restructure for the Audience

User: Restructure. Lead with the bottom line in the first sentence. Then list the three recommendations briefly. Then provide the supporting analysis. End with a single decision point we want leadership to address.

AI output: Restructured memo. Bottom line up front. Recommendations second. Analysis third. Decision point at end.

User notices: Almost there. The bottom line sentence is too soft. It says we should consider several actions. Leadership will not respond to consider.

Round 6: Sharpen Tone

User: Replace the bottom line sentence with one that takes a position rather than describing options. Make a recommendation that leadership can either accept or reject.

AI output: Bottom line now reads: We should test three retention bets in Q3 totaling approximately $200K, each targeting first six month churn among small customers.

User notices: That works. The memo feels strong. One last issue: the analysis section is still 200 words longer than it should be.

Round 7: Tighten Length

User: Cut the analysis section by 200 words while preserving the most important points. Combine related sentences. Remove any sentence that does not support the bottom line.

AI output: Tightened memo. The analysis section is leaner and more focused.

User notices: The whole memo now reads strong. One last polish: the closing decision point could be sharper.

Round 8: Final Polish

User: Replace the closing decision point with a single yes or no question for leadership. Specifically: are we authorized to allocate $200K in Q3 to test these three retention bets?

AI output: Final version of the memo with a clear yes or no closing question.

User notices: The memo is now exactly right. Eight rounds, but the result is dramatically better than what any single prompt could have produced. Total time spent: about 25 minutes.

Lessons From the Walkthrough

Several lessons emerge from this walkthrough. First, important deliverables often take many rounds. Eight rounds is not unusual for high stakes work. Second, each round addresses a specific issue. The user is not vaguely rewriting; they are surgically adjusting one dimension at a time. Third, the AI does not push back or volunteer improvements. The user must drive the iteration. The skill of driving iteration is the skill of prompting at the highest level.

> **Twenty Five Minutes That Saves Hours**
>
> Twenty five minutes of careful iteration produced a memo that would have taken several hours to write from scratch and gone through multiple human review cycles. The investment of careful iteration pays back many times over for important deliverables.

7.13 Building the Iteration Reflex

Iterative prompting is more habit than technique. The habit takes practice to develop. Below are exercises that help build the iteration reflex.

Exercise 1: The Three Round Minimum

For one week, commit to at least three rounds of iteration on every important AI output. Even if the first round looks fine, do at least two more refinements. Notice what you discover in the additional rounds. Most prompt writers find that what felt fine after one round was actually meaningfully improvable.

Exercise 2: The Targeted Change

For one week, every iteration must change exactly one thing. Length. Tone. Structure. Specificity. One dimension at a time. This forces you to diagnose what is actually wrong rather than vaguely rewriting. The discipline accelerates your diagnostic skill.

Exercise 3: The Critique Pattern

For one week, after every important first attempt, ask the AI to critique its own output before requesting any changes. Read the critique. Decide which parts you agree with. Then request the targeted changes. This pattern often surfaces issues you would have missed.

Exercise 4: The Audience Test

For one week, after every important output, ask yourself: would my actual audience find this useful as is? If not, what specifically would they push back on? Use the imagined pushback to drive the next round of iteration. This builds audience awareness into your workflow.

Exercise 5: The Save Habit

For one month, save every prompt that produces output you found genuinely useful. At the end of the month, you will have a small library of proven prompts. Review them. Notice patterns. Identify candidates for templates. The compounding has begun.

> *Iteration is the price of quality. Anyone willing to pay it can produce work that anyone unwilling to pay it cannot. The price is small. The discipline is the rare thing.*

Chapter 8: Improving Prompt Quality

By this point in the book, you have learned how prompts work, how to structure them, which design patterns to use, and how to apply foundational techniques like zero shot, few shot, step by step, and iterative prompting. This chapter steps back from technique and focuses on craft. How do you improve the quality of a prompt itself, beyond just selecting the right pattern or adding more context? What separates a workable prompt from an excellent one?

The answers lie in five areas. Recognizing weak prompts when you see them. Reducing vague language wherever it creeps in. Controlling tone and style with intention. Managing output length deliberately. And balancing precision with creativity in a way that fits the task. Each of these is a skill in its own right, and together they elevate the quality of every prompt you write.

8.1 Identifying Weak Prompts

The first step toward better prompts is recognizing weak ones. A weak prompt is not necessarily wrong. It is simply less effective than it could be. Weak prompts produce output that is acceptable but not great. The output works but does not shine. Identifying the weakness is the first move toward fixing it.

The Five Markers of a Weak Prompt

Weak prompts share recurring traits. Once you can spot them, you can repair them quickly. Five markers, in particular, are worth memorizing.

1. Vague verbs. Words like help me with, work on, or improve give the AI no specific action to take.
2. Missing audience. The prompt does not say who the output is for, leaving the AI to guess.
3. No format guidance. The prompt does not specify whether the output should be a list, a paragraph, a table, or something else.
4. Implicit context. The prompt refers to information the AI does not actually have, like the discussion we had yesterday or our usual style.
5. Mixed signals. The prompt asks for things that subtly conflict, like make this concise but detailed.

Each of these markers can appear individually or in combination. A prompt with one weakness may still produce decent output. A prompt with three or more is rolling dice. The repair is usually straightforward. Replace the vague verb with a specific one. Name the audience. Specify the format. Make the context explicit. Resolve the mixed signals into a single clear priority.

Before and After

Weak Prompt	Improved Prompt
Help me with this presentation.	Review the bullet points below for my five minute investor pitch and rewrite each one to be punchier and clearer for a non technical audience.
Make my email better.	Edit the email below for tone. Keep the message friendly but make the request clearer and remove any apologetic hedging.
Tell me about the meeting.	Summarize the meeting transcript below in 150 words for a colleague who missed the meeting. Highlight any decisions made and action items assigned.
Give me some marketing ideas.	Generate five low budget marketing ideas a solo founder of a software product could test in the first month after launch. Format as a numbered list with one sentence per idea.

Notice that the improved prompts are usually two to three times longer than the weak ones. They are also far more specific. The investment of an extra fifteen seconds of writing pays back many times over in the quality of the output. This is the trade you are making whenever you upgrade a weak prompt to a strong one. A small amount of extra effort up front for a much larger improvement in result.

8.2 Reducing Vague Language

Vague language is the single biggest enemy of prompt quality. Every vague word in a prompt forces the AI to interpret. Every interpretation is a guess. Every guess is a chance for the output to drift away from what you actually wanted. Reducing vague language, word by word, is one of the most reliable ways to improve any prompt.

Common Vague Words and How to Replace Them

Vague Word	Why It Is Vague	Concrete Replacement
good	What does good mean to you?	accurate, well organized, easy to scan, friendly
short	How short?	100 words, three sentences, one paragraph
long	How long?	five paragraphs, 800 words, a full page
professional	Whose professional standards?	in the tone of a corporate annual report
clear	Clear to whom?	understandable to a non technical reader
interesting	Interesting how?	with a surprising fact or unusual angle
natural	Natural in what register?	conversational, like a friendly text message
better	Better along which dimension?	more concise, more specific, easier to read

This table is not exhaustive, but it captures the most common offenders. Each replacement gives the AI a concrete target rather than a fuzzy aspiration. Concrete targets produce output that consistently lands closer to what you wanted.

The Vague Word Audit

A useful habit when writing important prompts is to do a quick vague word audit before sending. Read the prompt back and circle every word that could be interpreted multiple ways. For each circled word, ask whether you can replace it with something more concrete. Often you can. The replacement takes a few seconds. The output improvement is consistently noticeable.

> **Vague Language Test**
>
> After writing a prompt, ask yourself: if I gave this prompt to ten different people, how much would their interpretations of these words diverge? The bigger the divergence, the more vague the language. Tighten until the divergence shrinks to almost nothing.

8.3 Controlling Tone and Style

Tone and style are among the most subtle and impactful aspects of prompt design. Two pieces of writing can convey the same information yet feel completely different in tone. The AI is sensitive to tonal cues, but only when those cues are clear. Vague tonal direction produces output that drifts toward the AI's default voice, which is usually a generic helpful register that fits no specific use case perfectly.

Specifying Tone Effectively

Effective tone specification has two components. The first is direction, what kind of voice you want. The second is calibration, how much of that voice. Direction without calibration leaves the AI guessing. Saying friendly is a direction. Saying friendly but professional is direction with calibration. The AI now knows not just where to aim but how far to push.

Some of the most useful tone specifications are paired or opposing. Friendly but professional. Direct but warm. Confident but not arrogant. Encouraging but honest. Each pair captures a tonal balance that single words cannot. The AI uses both descriptors to triangulate the right register.

Style Versus Tone

Tone and style are related but distinct. Tone is the emotional register of writing. Style is the structural and stylistic choices that produce that register. Two writers might both have a friendly tone, but one achieves it through short punchy sentences and lots of contractions, while the other achieves it through carefully balanced longer sentences and warm vocabulary. Both are friendly, but their styles are different.

When you specify tone, the AI infers a style that fits. When you also specify style, you get more precise control. Examples of style specification include short sentences, no jargon, lots of concrete examples, frequent use of you to address the reader, no rhetorical questions, or one paragraph per idea. Each style choice constrains the AI in a way that produces output more aligned with how you want it to sound.

Examples to Match Tone

Sometimes the best way to specify tone and style is through examples. Few shot prompting, introduced in Chapter 5, applies here too. Provide a paragraph or two of writing that demonstrates the tone and style you want. Then ask the AI to produce new content in the same voice. The AI will pattern match against the example far better than it can match against verbal description alone.

```
Here is an example of the tone I want my product update emails to use:  "Hey
team, quick update on the Kepler launch. We shipped the photo upload fix
yesterday, and the crash rate is already down by 80 percent. Big thanks to Maria
and Devon for tracking it down. Next up: the search bug. Aiming for end of
```

```
week."  Using that same tone, write a product update email about the dashboard
redesign that shipped this morning. The redesign cleans up the navigation, adds
a search bar, and renames a few menu items. Marcus and Priya led the work.
```

This kind of prompt produces output that sounds remarkably like the example. The AI captures not just the words but the rhythm, the warmth, the brevity, the specific pattern of crediting team members. Tone matching by example is one of the most powerful techniques you can use for any work where voice matters.

8.4 Managing Output Length

Length is often treated as an afterthought, but it deserves attention. The right length is not just a matter of word count. It is a matter of fit. A 200 word answer to a question that needed 50 wastes the reader's time. A 50 word answer to a question that needed 500 leaves them unsatisfied. Calibrating length to the task is part of the craft.

How to Specify Length Precisely

AI models respond to explicit length instructions reliably, but not perfectly. They tend to slightly overshoot or undershoot, especially for very short or very long targets. Several specification techniques produce more consistent results.

1. Specify in multiple units. Saying 200 words or about three short paragraphs gives the AI two anchors that reinforce each other.
2. Specify a range. Saying 150 to 200 words is more flexible than saying exactly 175 words and produces output that sits more naturally in the target zone.
3. Specify by structure. Saying five bullet points, each one sentence is more reliable than saying about 100 words because the structure constrains length naturally.
4. Specify maximum, not exact. Saying no more than 300 words tends to produce output near 280, which is often what you actually wanted.
5. For long output, specify section sizes. A 1500 word essay with five sections of about 300 words each is more reliable than just a 1500 word essay.

Common Length Pitfalls

A few length related pitfalls show up often. The first is asking for a brief overview when you really wanted depth. Brief and overview are vague, so the AI defaults to a short generic response. The second is asking for a comprehensive treatment when you really wanted a quick summary. Comprehensive triggers long output, which may overshoot the readers attention budget. The third is using qualitative length words like detailed or thorough without quantifying. Detailed to one person is excessive to another.

The cure for all of these pitfalls is the same. Replace qualitative length descriptions with quantitative ones. Specific numbers, sentence counts, paragraph counts, or section structures. Each of these takes the guesswork out of length and makes output reliably the size you wanted.

8.5 Precision Versus Creativity Balance

The final dimension of prompt quality is something we will call the precision creativity balance. Some tasks demand precision. The output must be exact, accurate, and conform to specific standards. Other tasks demand creativity. The output must be original, surprising, or imaginative. Most tasks sit somewhere on a spectrum between the two. Knowing where on the spectrum your task sits, and writing a prompt that matches, is the highest level skill in this chapter.

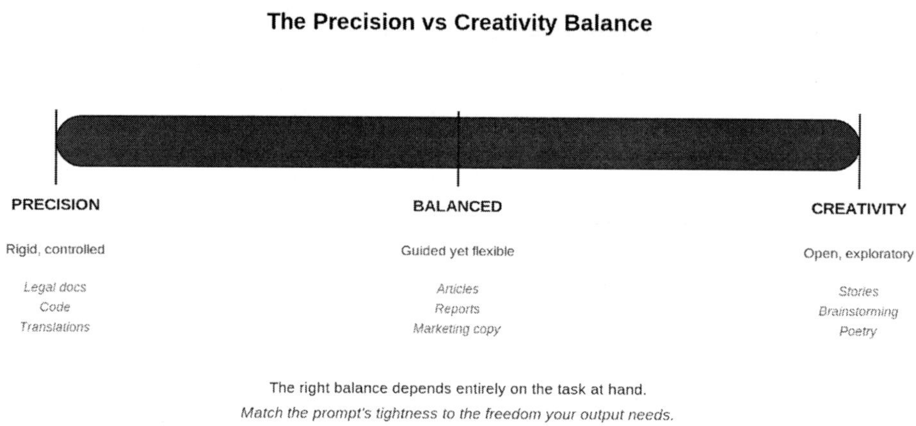

Figure 8.1: The precision creativity spectrum and the kinds of work that fall on each end.

Precision Heavy Tasks

Precision heavy tasks include legal drafting, technical writing, code, translations of documents that must be accurate, regulatory writing, financial analysis, and any task where being wrong has real consequences. Prompts for precision heavy tasks should be tightly constrained. Specify exactly what to include and what to exclude. Provide source material the AI must rely on rather than inventing. Ask the AI to flag uncertainty rather than fill in gaps with plausible guesses. Forbid invention of facts, statistics, or names. Use few shot examples to lock in format.

In precision heavy work, creativity is not your friend. The AI's creative tendencies must be reined in deliberately. Phrases like only use information from the source provided, do not invent statistics, and if uncertain, say so explicitly are essential. Without them, the AI may produce output that reads beautifully but contains fabricated content.

Creativity Heavy Tasks

Creativity heavy tasks include fiction writing, brainstorming, naming exercises, marketing copy, exploratory analysis, and any task where novelty and imagination matter more than strict accuracy. Prompts for creative tasks should be looser, leaving room for the AI to surprise you. Specify the constraints that matter, like length and audience, but leave open the parts that benefit from creative freedom.

Over constraining a creative prompt can backfire. If you specify too much, the output becomes formulaic. If you specify the structure, the tone, the topic, the angle, the metaphors, and the ending all at once, you have left the AI no room to breathe. Counterintuitively, sometimes the best creative prompts are the loosest, asking for many variations and letting you pick from them.

Mixed Tasks

Most real world tasks are mixed. A marketing campaign needs precision in factual claims and creativity in voice. A product description needs accuracy about the product and imagination about the appeal. A help article needs technical correctness and accessible style. For these tasks, prompts must walk the line, specifying what must be precise and what can be free.

A useful pattern is to label which parts are precision and which are creative. For example, the bullet points listing features must be factually accurate based on the spec sheet provided. The opening tagline can be creative and surprising, prioritizing memorability over completeness. The AI can then apply different standards to different parts of the same output, exactly the way a human writer would.

> **Balance Self Test**
>
> For any prompt, ask: does the AI need to be more accurate or more imaginative here? Most prompts privilege one over the other. Naming which side you want is a small move with outsized effects on quality.

8.6 Chapter Recap

This chapter focused on the craft of improving prompts beyond just structure and pattern.

- Identify weak prompts by looking for vague verbs, missing audiences, no format guidance, implicit context, and mixed signals.
- Reduce vague language by replacing words like good, short, professional, and better with concrete equivalents.

- Control tone and style with paired descriptors, style specification, and tone matching examples drawn from real writing.
- Manage output length with specific numbers, ranges, structural constraints, and section sizes for longer output.
- Balance precision and creativity by labeling which parts of the output need accuracy and which benefit from imagination.

Practice Exercise

This audit converts the five markers of weak prompts into a routine you can run on any prompt before you send it.

1. Pull up five prompts you have used recently. Real prompts from real work, not invented ones.
2. Read each prompt against the five markers of weak prompts: vague verbs, missing audience, no format guidance, implicit context, and mixed signals.
3. Note which markers each prompt commits. Most prompts will commit at least one.
4. Rewrite each prompt to fix the weaknesses you identified.
5. Run both versions of each prompt and compare the outputs.

The pattern you will notice across all five is that the rewrites consistently produce output that lands closer to what you wanted on the first try, which means less iteration and faster results overall.

8.7 The Anatomy of a Weak Prompt: A Detailed Walkthrough

Section 8.1 listed five markers of weak prompts. This expansion walks through a detailed before and after, examining each marker in context and showing how the repair affects output.

The Original Prompt

```
Help me with my pitch deck. Make it better.
```

This prompt has every marker of weakness packed into eleven words. Vague verb (help me with, make better). Missing audience (pitch deck for whom?). No format guidance. Implicit context (the AI does not know what pitch deck). Mixed signals (help and make better could mean entirely different things).

First Repair: Specify the Verb

```
Review my pitch deck and identify the three biggest weaknesses.
```

Better. Now there is a clear verb (review) and a specific output (three weaknesses). But the AI still does not know what kind of pitch deck, who it is for, or what better means.

Second Repair: Add Audience

```
Review my pitch deck and identify the three biggest weaknesses. The deck is for
a Series A pitch to early stage investors who care most about market size and
traction.
```

Now the audience is concrete. The AI knows what investors care about. The weaknesses it identifies will be specifically about market size signals and traction evidence rather than generic deck advice.

Third Repair: Add Format

```
Review my pitch deck and identify the three biggest weaknesses. The deck is for
a Series A pitch to early stage investors who care most about market size and
traction.  For each weakness, produce: a one sentence statement of the issue, a
one sentence explanation of why it matters to investors, and a one sentence
suggested fix.  Format as a numbered list with three items.
```

Now the structure is locked in. The AI knows the exact shape of the response. Each weakness gets equal treatment. The output will be scannable, comparable, and actionable.

Fourth Repair: Add the Source Material

Of course, the AI cannot review a deck it has not seen. The final repair is to attach the deck content.

```
[The complete repaired prompt now includes a link to or transcript of the deck
content. Without it, the AI has no source to review.]
```

This walkthrough illustrates the cumulative effect of small repairs. None of them is dramatic on its own. Together they transform a vague request into a precise instruction that produces actionable output. Each repair takes seconds. The total investment of a minute or two pays back many times over.

8.8 Vague Language Vocabulary Expansion

Section 8.2 listed common vague words. This expansion provides a much fuller catalog and discusses why each is vague and what concrete alternatives work better.

Vague Word	Why It Is Vague	Examples of Concrete Alternatives
effective	Effective at what? Measured how?	achieves the stated goal, increases conversion by X percent
robust	Robust against what?	handles malformed input gracefully, scales to 1000 concurrent users
scalable	Scalable in what dimension?	supports up to 10,000 records, accommodates ten times current users
simple	Simple to whom?	requires no setup steps, fits in a single screen
clean	Clean by what standard?	follows our style guide, uses no unused imports
intuitive	Intuitive to whom?	discoverable within thirty seconds for a first time user
actionable	What action?	specifies who does what by when
high quality	Quality by which standard?	matches the editorial standards of our flagship publication
polished	Polished how?	no typos, consistent voice, balanced section lengths
compelling	Compelling to whom?	resonates with first time founders considering raising capital
thoughtful	Thoughtful in what way?	considers second order effects, surfaces trade offs explicitly
modern	Modern by what reference point?	uses 2024 best practices in front end design
best	Best by what criterion?	highest expected user satisfaction given the budget

Vague Word	Why It Is Vague	Examples of Concrete Alternatives
right	Right for whom?	fits a small team without a dedicated DevOps engineer
solid	Solid in what dimension?	tested with at least 80 percent code coverage

This catalog is not exhaustive but covers the words that most often weaken prompts in business and creative writing. Whenever you find one of these in your prompt, ask whether you can replace it with a concrete equivalent. Most of the time, you can. The output will follow.

8.9 Tone and Style: A Working Library

Section 8.3 covered tone and style. This expansion offers a working library of tone descriptions and style choices that you can mix and match for different tasks.

Tone Descriptors by Category

Category	Tone Words	Best For
Warm	warm, friendly, welcoming, gentle, kind	Customer interactions, internal communications, education
Cool	neutral, measured, dispassionate, calm, even	Technical writing, legal documents, analysis
Direct	direct, plain spoken, clear, no nonsense, blunt	Internal team updates, urgent messages, instructions
Formal	formal, professional, polished, refined, elevated	Executive communications, contracts, public statements
Casual	casual, conversational, breezy, relaxed, off the cuff	Marketing copy, blog posts, internal Slack
Energetic	energetic, enthusiastic, vibrant, lively, spirited	Product launches, motivational content, marketing

Category	Tone Words	Best For
Serious	serious, grave, weighty, sober, deliberate	Crisis communications, sensitive topics, formal apologies
Playful	playful, witty, light, whimsical, mischievous	Brand voice, social media, copy with personality
Encouraging	encouraging, supportive, hopeful, affirming	Education, coaching, internal pep talks
Skeptical	skeptical, cautious, critical, questioning, doubting	Analysis, critical reviews, devil's advocate

Style Choices Beyond Tone

Tone is the emotional register. Style is the structural and lexical choices that create that register. The same tone can be achieved through very different styles. Below are common style dimensions you can specify alongside tone.

- Sentence length. Short sentences for punch and clarity. Long sentences for reflective or formal registers.
- Vocabulary level. Simple everyday words for accessibility. Specialized vocabulary for expert audiences.
- Use of contractions. Contractions (it is, do not) for casual. Avoidance for formal.
- Pronoun choice. You for direct address. We for collective. They for distance.
- Active versus passive voice. Active for energy. Passive for distance or when the actor does not matter.
- Use of metaphors and analogies. Many for accessibility. Few for precision.
- Sentence variety. Mixing lengths and structures for rhythm. Repetition of structure for formality.
- Use of questions. Rhetorical questions for engagement. Statements for authority.
- Use of humor. Welcomed in casual contexts. Avoided in serious or sensitive contexts.
- Direct address. Speaking to the reader directly. Or maintaining narrative distance.

Specifying both tone and a few style choices produces output much more aligned with what you actually want. Each dimension narrows the possibility space. Together they zero in on a specific voice that fits the moment.

8.10 Length Specification in Detail

Section 8.4 covered managing output length. This expansion looks at length in finer detail, with attention to the specific units of measurement that work best for different kinds of output.

Units of Length

Unit	Best For	Reliability
Words	Articles, summaries, descriptions	High, especially in 100 to 500 range
Sentences	Single ideas, captions, summaries	Very high
Paragraphs	Articles, essays, structured prose	High
Bullets	Lists, action items, takeaways	Very high
Sections	Reports, documents	High when sections are named
Pages	Long documents	Low, varies by formatting
Characters	Tweets, headlines, constrained interfaces	Moderate, may be approximate
Tokens	Programmatic use	Imprecise; AI tokens differ from word counts

Length Anchoring Techniques

AI models do not always hit length targets exactly. Several techniques produce more reliable length matching.

1. Specify a range, not a point. 200 to 250 words produces output that lands in that range much more reliably than exactly 225 words.
2. Combine units. 200 words or roughly three paragraphs gives the AI two anchors that reinforce each other.
3. Specify by structure. Three sections, each two paragraphs of about 100 words is more reliable than one length specification.
4. Provide a length example. Length should match the example below in volume. The example does the work that a number cannot.

5. State both maximum and minimum when both matter. At least 100 words and no more than 200 produces output in that range.

8.11 The Precision Creativity Tradeoff: Expanded

Section 8.5 introduced the precision creativity balance. This expansion looks at common task categories and where each typically falls on the spectrum, with prompt structures suited to each zone.

Maximum Precision Zone

Tasks that require maximum precision include legal contract drafting, medical information, financial calculations, code that must execute correctly, technical documentation, regulatory filings, and translations of formal documents. For these tasks, prompts should be tightly constrained, source bound, and explicitly instructed to flag uncertainty.

Sample structure for maximum precision tasks. Use only the source material below. Do not invent facts, names, or numbers. If any information is not present in the source, say so explicitly. Format the output as [specific format]. Length: [specific limit]. Style: [specific style guide reference if available].

High Precision Zone

Tasks that require high precision include research summaries, business reports, professional emails, code reviews, instructional content, and product descriptions. For these tasks, prompts should be specific about facts but allow some interpretation in language and emphasis.

Balanced Zone

Tasks in the balanced zone include articles, blog posts, marketing copy, presentations, executive summaries, and most everyday writing tasks. For these tasks, prompts should specify the audience, format, length, and tone, but leave room for the AI to make interpretive choices about emphasis and language.

High Creativity Zone

Tasks in the high creativity zone include creative writing exercises, naming and ideation, brand storytelling, social media content, and exploratory brainstorming. For these tasks, prompts should set creative constraints (themes, audience, tone) but leave the actual creative choices open.

Maximum Creativity Zone

Tasks at maximum creativity include fiction, poetry, art prompts, comedy writing, and pure idea generation. For these tasks, prompts should provide direction and inspiration but minimal constraints. Over constraining creative work produces output that feels by the book rather than alive.

> **Match the Zone**
>
> Before writing any prompt, ask which zone the task belongs in. Match the prompt's tightness to the zone. Loose prompts for creative work. Tight prompts for precision work. The match itself is one of the most consequential decisions you make.

8.12 Five Case Studies in Prompt Improvement

To consolidate the principles of this chapter, here are five case studies showing how a weak prompt evolves into a strong one through deliberate improvement. Each case study includes the original prompt, the analysis of its weaknesses, and the improved version.

Case Study 1: A Vague Email Request

Original. Help me reply to this customer email.

Analysis. The verb help is vague. There is no audience or stakes information. There is no length or format guidance. The customer email is implicitly referenced but not provided in the prompt structure.

Improved. Draft a reply to the customer email below. The customer is upset that their order was delayed by a week. They paid extra for express shipping. Acknowledge the issue, apologize sincerely without grovelling, offer a refund of the express shipping fee, and reassure them that we have addressed the underlying cause. Tone should be warm and accountable. Length: under 150 words. Format as a complete email with subject line, body, and signature line. [Customer email below.]

Case Study 2: A Generic Marketing Brief

Original. Write some marketing copy for our app.

Analysis. The verb is fine but everything else is missing. The audience, format, length, app details, target action, brand voice are all unspecified.

Improved. Write a 75 word marketing description of our productivity app for the App Store listing. The audience is busy parents who want to track family schedules and grocery lists in one place. The app is called HearthHub. The brand voice is warm, honest, and lightly humorous, like a good neighbor giving advice. Include one specific feature mention (shared grocery lists synced across phones) and end with a call to action to download free.

Case Study 3: An Underdescribed Code Task

Original. Write me a script that reads the file.

Analysis. Which language? What kind of file? What format? What should it do with the contents? What are the inputs and outputs? Almost everything is missing.

Improved. Write a Python script that reads a CSV file from a path provided as a command line argument. The CSV has the columns name, email, signup_date, and active (true or false). The script should print the count of active users, the count of inactive users, and the email addresses of users who signed up in the last 30 days. Include error handling for missing files and malformed rows. Include a docstring at the top of the script.

Case Study 4: A Bare Analysis Request

Original. Analyze our quarterly numbers.

Analysis. There is no source material, no audience, no analytical lens, no output format, no length guidance, no specific question.

Improved. Acting as a financial analyst, analyze the quarterly numbers in the table below. The audience is the executive team, who care about top line growth, gross margin trends, and customer acquisition cost. Identify the three most significant trends across the four quarters and the one trend that most concerns you. Format as four labeled paragraphs (one per significant trend, plus the concerning one). Length: roughly 75 words per paragraph.

Case Study 5: A Vague Brainstorm

Original. Give me ideas for our team event.

Analysis. The team size, budget, location, time available, what kind of event, what we are trying to achieve are all unspecified. The output format is also unspecified.

Improved. Generate eight ideas for an in person team event for our 12 person engineering team. Budget: $500 total. Duration: half a day. Location: walking distance from our office in midtown Manhattan. Goal: build connection across recently merged sub teams who do not yet know each other well. Format as a numbered list. For each idea, include a one sentence description and a one sentence rationale tied to our goal of building connection.

In each case, the improved prompt is two to four times longer than the original, but it produces output that lands much closer to what was actually wanted. The investment is worth it for any task where the output matters.

8.13 The Quality Improvement Catalog

Below is a working catalog of techniques for improving prompt output quality, organized by what they do. Use this as a reference. When output is not what you want, find the relevant section and apply the corresponding technique.

Techniques That Sharpen Substance

- Add concrete context. Replace abstract framing with specific details about your situation.
- Provide source material. Bind the AI to specific facts rather than letting it generate from training.
- Specify what is in scope and out of scope. Explicit boundaries prevent drift.
- Ask for specific evidence. Require the AI to point to support for its claims.
- Request alternatives. Ask for two or three options rather than one, and the AI will think more carefully.

Techniques That Sharpen Structure

- Specify the format explicitly. Lists, tables, sections, paragraphs.
- Provide a skeleton to fill in. The AI follows skeletons more reliably than verbal descriptions.
- Specify the size of each section. Otherwise the AI distributes attention unevenly.
- Order sections explicitly. Do not let the AI choose the order if it matters.
- Use few shot examples to lock in custom formats. Verbal descriptions are weaker than examples.

Techniques That Sharpen Style

- Pair tonal descriptors. Warm but professional, direct but kind, confident but humble.
- Provide voice examples. A paragraph of writing in the voice you want teaches the AI more than ten words of description.
- Specify what the voice is not. Not formal, not stiff, not corporate. Negation directs the AI away from defaults.
- Specify style choices alongside tone. Sentence length, vocabulary level, contractions.

- Use a brand voice reference if your work has one. Aligns with established norms efficiently.

Techniques That Sharpen Length

- Specify length in multiple units. 200 words or roughly three paragraphs.
- Specify length per section. Otherwise the AI distributes unevenly.
- Use ranges, not exact numbers. 200 to 250 words is more reliable than exactly 225.
- State maximum and minimum if both matter.
- Specify by structure when length specification fails. Three bullets, each one sentence is more reliable than 60 words.

Techniques That Sharpen Audience Fit

- Name the audience specifically. Not just business people but mid level managers in the manufacturing sector.
- Describe the audience's expertise level. Affects vocabulary and depth.
- Describe the audience's emotional state. Affects tone.
- Describe the audience's time pressure. Affects length and structure.
- Describe what the audience cares about most. Aligns the output's emphasis.

Techniques That Reduce Common Errors

- Bind to source material to reduce hallucination. Use only the document below.
- Ask for uncertainty flags. Surfaces gaps the AI would otherwise hide.
- Verify high stakes claims externally. AI is a starting point, not a source.
- Use few shot examples for high consistency tasks. Examples lock in patterns reliably.
- Reset conversations that have wandered. Fresh starts often beat continued recovery attempts.

The Pattern Library

These techniques together form a working pattern library you can draw from. Most output quality issues fall into one or two categories. Knowing which technique to reach for is what makes iteration fast and effective.

8.14 Twenty More Case Studies in Prompt Improvement

Section 8.12 included five case studies. Below are twenty more, ranging across professional, personal, and creative tasks. Read several. Notice the patterns. The same kinds of repairs work across very different content domains.

Case 6: Performance Review

Original: Write a performance review for one of my reports.

Improved: Draft a balanced six month review for a senior software engineer on my team. Strengths: technical depth, mentorship of juniors, code quality. Growth areas: cross functional communication and willingness to disagree productively. Tone: warm but candid. Length: 350 words. Format: three labeled sections (Strengths, Growth Areas, Goals for Next Period). Include specific observable behaviors rather than abstract assessments.

Case 7: Difficult Conversation Prep

Original: Help me prepare to talk to my employee about being late.

Improved: Help me prepare for a one on one conversation with a direct report about chronic lateness (three or more late arrivals per week for the past month). My goals are to understand any underlying cause, set a clear expectation going forward, and preserve the relationship. Provide a suggested opening, three open ended questions, and a possible close. Tone should be direct but warm.

Case 8: Sales Outreach

Original: Write a sales email.

Improved: Write a 100 word cold email to the head of operations at a mid sized logistics company. The pitch is for our route optimization software. Open with a specific operational pain (driver hours wasted on inefficient routes). Make a clear hypothesis about how this likely affects their company. Close with an offer of a 20 minute conversation, not a demo. Tone: confident but not pushy.

Case 9: Investor Update

Original: Write a quarterly investor update.

Improved: Write a quarterly investor update for a Series A SaaS company. Q3 highlights: revenue grew 22 percent quarter over quarter, churn flat at 8 percent annual, hired three engineers and a head of marketing. Q3 challenges: enterprise sales cycle lengthening from 60 to 95 days. Tone: confident, transparent, no spin. Length: 400 words. Format: Bottom line up front, then sections Highlights, Challenges, Asks of Investors.

Case 10: Personal Blog Post

Original: Write a blog post about productivity.

Improved: Write a 500 word personal blog post arguing that most productivity advice misses the importance of unstructured thinking time. Voice: conversational, slightly opinionated, willing to push back on conventional wisdom. Open with a specific moment of tension between scheduled work and free thinking. Use one personal example. End with a single concrete suggestion for readers.

Case 11: Wedding Toast

Original: Write a wedding toast for my brother.

Improved: Write a 90 second wedding toast for my younger brother. He is marrying someone I have known for three years. Specific things to mention: he is the more disciplined sibling, his fiancee is the funniest person he knows, they met when they were both volunteering at an animal shelter. Tone: warm, lightly funny, not sentimental. End with a toast that fits this couple specifically.

Case 12: Customer Apology

Original: Apology email to customer.

Improved: Draft a 120 word apology to a customer whose order was delayed by ten days due to our shipping vendor's system outage. Acknowledge the delay clearly without excessive apologizing. State what we are doing for them (full refund of shipping plus a $20 store credit). State what we are doing to prevent recurrence (switching primary shipping vendor next month). Tone: accountable, warm, no corporate speak.

Case 13: Product Hunt Description

Original: Description for Product Hunt launch.

Improved: Write a 60 word Product Hunt tagline and description for our new AI writing assistant. Audience: indie hackers and small team founders. Hook: the assistant focuses on substance over style, refusing to bloat short emails into long ones. Tone: confident, slightly counterintuitive, no buzzwords like revolutionize or transform.

Case 14: Newsletter Subject Line

Original: Help with newsletter subject lines.

Improved: Generate ten subject lines for a weekly newsletter about indie business. The audience is solopreneurs and small team founders. Tone should be warm and slightly insider, not corporate.

Each subject line should be under 50 characters. Avoid generic words like update, weekly, and newsletter. Lean toward specific, curiosity inducing phrasing.

Case 15: Conference Abstract

Original: Write a talk abstract for a conference.

Improved: Write a 150 word abstract for a 30 minute talk at a regional engineering conference. Topic: lessons from migrating our monolith to microservices, including the surprises (both good and bad). Audience: senior engineers who have heard many microservices talks. The abstract should signal that this talk has fresh content, not generic best practices. Open with the most counterintuitive lesson.

Case 16: Sympathy Card

Original: Write a sympathy card to a coworker.

Improved: Write a 40 word handwritten card to a coworker whose father passed away last week. We are friendly but not close. Tone: warm, brief, not religious. Avoid cliches like sorry for your loss. Acknowledge the loss without trying to fix anything. End with a specific small offer of support.

Case 17: Restaurant Review

Original: Review a restaurant I went to.

Improved: Write a 200 word restaurant review for a small Italian place I visited last weekend. The pasta was excellent, the service was friendly but slow, the room was loud. Voice: honest and warm, not snobbish. Audience: people considering a casual dinner spot. End with a clear recommendation: who would enjoy this place and who probably should not.

Case 18: Resignation Email

Original: Email to resign.

Improved: Draft a 90 word resignation email to my manager. Tenure: three years. Reason: accepted a senior role at another company. I want to leave on excellent terms. Include the date of my last day (two weeks from today), an offer to help transition my projects, and a brief note of appreciation. Tone: warm and grateful, not gushing.

Case 19: Data Insight Memo

Original: Memo about user data.

Improved: Write a 300 word memo summarizing the user behavior data below for the product team. Three labeled sections: What We Saw, What We Think It Means, What We Recommend.

Lean on the data. Be explicit about what is interpretation versus what is observation. Recommendations should be testable hypotheses, not certainties.

Case 20: Job Interview Question Prep

Original: Help me prep for an interview.

Improved: Help me prepare for behavioral interview questions for a senior product manager role at a B2B SaaS company. Generate ten likely questions, and for each, sketch the structure of a strong answer using the STAR method (Situation, Task, Action, Result). My background: six years of PM experience at two startups, with strengths in customer development and weaknesses in formal data analysis.

Case 21: Bug Report

Original: Help me write a bug report.

Improved: Write a clear bug report for the engineering team. Title format: short description of the symptom. Sections: Steps to Reproduce (numbered list), Expected Behavior, Actual Behavior, Environment Details, Severity (high, medium, low with rationale). Lean on specifics. Avoid speculation about root cause.

Case 22: Apology to a Friend

Original: Apologize to my friend.

Improved: Draft an apology text to a friend whose birthday I forgot last week. We have been close for years. Acknowledge the lapse without making excuses. Take responsibility. Suggest specifically how to make it up (offer to take her to dinner this weekend). Tone: warm, slightly self deprecating, not groveling. Length: under 60 words.

Case 23: Customer Survey

Original: Make me a customer survey.

Improved: Design a 5 question customer satisfaction survey for users of our project management software. Goal: identify the top friction point in their daily use. Mix of question types: one likert scale, one multiple choice, one ranking, two open ended. Include skip logic where appropriate. Estimated completion time: under 90 seconds.

Case 24: Gift Idea Brainstorm

Original: Suggest gift ideas for my dad.

Improved: Suggest eight gift ideas for my dad's 70th birthday. He is retired, an avid reader of history, gardens on weekends, and mildly resistant to new technology. Budget: $50 to $150. Lean toward thoughtful items that show personal attention rather than generic choices. Avoid gadgets, gift cards, and anything that requires app setup.

Case 25: Podcast Pitch

Original: Pitch myself for a podcast.

Improved: Draft a 100 word pitch email to a podcast host I admire. Their show is about indie business. My angle: I am a solo founder who built a $40K MRR SaaS product with no funding. I want to share three specific tactical lessons that go against conventional wisdom. Open with a specific reference to one of their recent episodes that resonated with me. Close with a clear ask: a 30 minute interview. Tone: warm and confident, not salesy.

8.15 Tone Library: Worked Examples Across Twenty Tones

To make tonal direction more concrete, below are twenty tones with example output for each. The same content (a paragraph announcing a delayed product launch) takes on dramatically different feeling across tones. Read several. Notice how vocabulary, sentence length, and emphasis shift.

Tone 1: Warm and Honest

Quick update friends. The new edition is going to be a bit late. Our printer ran into a paper shortage that nobody saw coming, and rather than cut corners, we decided to wait for the right paper. New ship date is the 15th. Thanks for your patience. We promise it is going to be worth the wait.

Tone 2: Confident and Direct

The new edition will ship on the 15th, two weeks behind the original date. The cause was a paper shortage at our printer. We chose to wait for our usual paper rather than substitute. Tracking emails will go out on ship day.

Tone 3: Urgent but Calm

Important update on the launch. We are now targeting the 15th rather than the 1st. The delay is from a printer side paper shortage. We are not changing the spec. Watch for tracking emails on ship day.

Tone 4: Apologetic

We are so sorry about this. The new edition is going to be two weeks late. Our printer hit a paper shortage we did not anticipate, and we know that affects everyone who has been waiting. Please bear with us. New ship date: the 15th. Thank you for your patience.

Tone 5: Witty

Plot twist: the new edition needs another two weeks. Our printer is short on paper, which is a problem when you make books. We chose to wait for the good stuff rather than ship something we would regret. Mark the 15th. Thanks for the extra patience.

Tone 6: Corporate

We are writing to inform you of an updated shipment timeline for the new edition. Due to a supply chain disruption affecting paper availability at our printing partner, the original ship date of the 1st has been adjusted to the 15th. We appreciate your understanding.

Tone 7: Plain Spoken

Heads up. The new edition is going to be late. Two extra weeks. Our printer is short on the right paper and we did not want to ship on the wrong stuff. New date: the 15th. More info on tracking when we send the books out.

Tone 8: Reflective

Sometimes things take longer than you planned. The new edition is one of those. Our printer hit an unexpected paper shortage, and we made the call to wait. Quality matters more than speed in this business. We will ship on the 15th, two weeks later than we hoped.

Tone 9: Encouraging

The wait is almost over. We know the new edition has been a long time coming, and we are now two weeks behind even our adjusted timeline because of a paper shortage at our printer. We promise: it is going to be worth it. Ship date: the 15th.

Tone 10: Skeptical of Self

Quick update, and we will be honest, this is the second timeline change for this launch. The printer hit a paper shortage. We are now targeting the 15th. We have not nailed launches as crisply as we would like. We are working on that. Thanks for sticking with us.

Tone 11: Energetic

Two more weeks! That is the news. Paper shortage at our printer is pushing the new edition launch to the 15th. We know, we know. But the books are going to be beautiful. Tracking emails go out on ship day. Get ready.

Tone 12: Serious

There has been a delay in the production of the new edition. A paper shortage at our printer means we are now targeting a ship date of the 15th. We considered shipping with a substitute paper but decided that did not meet the standard we set for this product.

Tone 13: Conversational

Hey, quick news. The new edition is going to be late. Like two weeks late. Our printer is having a paper problem, and we did not want to switch to the wrong paper just to hit the original date. So we are looking at the 15th now. Tracking goes out then. Thanks for waiting.

Tone 14: Formal

Dear customer, we wish to inform you of a change to the shipping timeline for the new edition. Owing to a paper shortage at our printer, the ship date has been revised from the 1st to the 15th. We appreciate your continued patience.

Tone 15: Empathetic

We know waiting is hard, especially when you have already been waiting a while. The new edition is going to be two weeks later than we said. The reason is a paper shortage at our printer. We made the call to wait for the right paper rather than substitute. New date: the 15th.

Tone 16: Brief

New edition delayed two weeks. Paper shortage at printer. Ships the 15th.

Tone 17: Detailed

We have an update on the new edition. Our printer informed us last Thursday that they have run into a paper shortage affecting our specific paper. After evaluating substitute options, we decided that none met our quality standards for this edition. We have rescheduled production for the 8th, which puts the ship date at the 15th. Tracking emails will go out the morning of ship day.

Tone 18: Reassuring

No need to worry. The new edition is on its way. We are running about two weeks behind because of a paper shortage at our printer, but everything else is on track. We will ship on the 15th. The books will be exactly as we promised.

Tone 19: Storytelling

Last Thursday, the printer called. They were out of our paper. The thing about our paper is that it is what makes the book feel like the book. Without it, the project becomes something else. So we waited. The new ship date is the 15th. The wait will be worth it.

Tone 20: Action Oriented

Update: New edition ships the 15th, two weeks later than planned. Cause: paper shortage at printer. Action: continuing with our usual paper rather than substituting. Next steps for you: nothing required. Tracking emails go out on ship day.

Notice how each tone handles the same information differently. Sentence length shifts. Vocabulary changes. Emphasis lands in different places. Choosing the right tone for the right audience is one of the highest leverage moves in any communication. Saying the right thing badly can be worse than saying nothing. Saying the right thing in the right tone is what gets work done.

Chapter 9: Troubleshooting and Best Practices

Even with strong technique, AI outputs sometimes go wrong. The output may be irrelevant, incomplete, factually shaky, or inconsistent across attempts. This chapter is about diagnosis and repair. We will walk through the most common failure modes, the likely causes of each, and the techniques that correct them. We will then close with a list of do's and don'ts that captures the working habits of effective prompt writers.

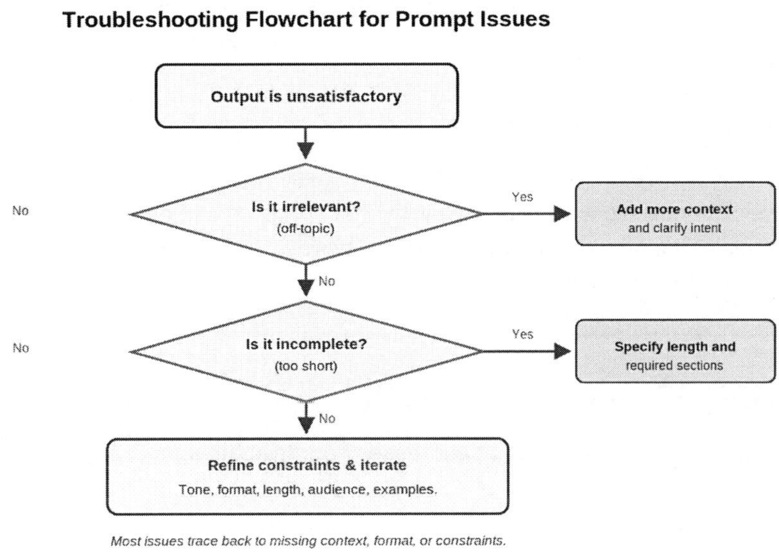

Figure 9.1: A troubleshooting flowchart for common prompt issues.

9.1 Fixing Irrelevant Outputs

An irrelevant output is one that is on a related topic but does not actually answer your question or complete your task. The AI talks around your request rather than at it. This is one of the most frustrating failure modes because the output looks competent on the surface, but it does not move you forward.

Why Irrelevance Happens

Irrelevance has three common causes. The first is that the prompt is too vague, leaving the AI to choose its own angle. It chose one. You did not want that one. The second is that the prompt mixes multiple requests, and the AI focused on the wrong one. The third is that the prompt referred to context the AI does not actually have, so it filled the gap with its own interpretation.

How to Fix Irrelevance

The repair depends on the cause. For vagueness, sharpen the instruction and add the missing context. For mixed requests, separate them into different prompts or label which is primary. For missing context, supply the context explicitly within the prompt itself. In every case, the principle is the same. Reduce the AI's need to guess.

A useful technique when irrelevance keeps occurring is to add a do statement near the end of the prompt that names the desired output explicitly. Phrases like the output should be a single recommendation, the response should focus only on questions of pricing, or the answer should be limited to the technical implementation force the AI back onto the path you want.

> **Reset Prompt for Irrelevance**
>
> When the AI keeps drifting off topic, do not chase it with follow ups. Reset the conversation. Write a fresh prompt with the explicit topic, the explicit boundaries, and an example of the kind of answer you want. The reset usually produces better output than continuing to refine a derailed thread.

9.2 Handling Incomplete Answers

An incomplete answer is one that addresses your task but stops short of fully completing it. You asked for five ideas, you got three. You asked for a thorough review, you got a paragraph. You asked for code with comments, you got code with no explanation. The output is not wrong, just thin.

Why Answers Come Up Short

Incomplete answers usually have one of three causes. The first is that the prompt did not specify the expected scope clearly. The AI made a reasonable guess about how much to produce, and that guess was less than you wanted. The second is that the AI hit a length boundary, either real or trained, and stopped early. The third is that the prompt asked for too many things, and the AI rationed its attention across them, giving each one only a partial treatment.

How to Fix Incompleteness

For scope issues, specify the expected scope explicitly. Five ideas means five, not three or seven. Each section must be at least 200 words means each section is at least 200 words. Numbers turn vague expectations into measurable targets that the AI can hit.

For length boundary issues, you can ask for output in chunks. Write the first half of the analysis, then stop. The next prompt asks for the second half. The AI is freed from compressing everything into a single response. For prompts asking too many things, separate them. Multiple prompts each focused on one task tend to produce more complete results than one prompt asking for ten things.

The Continuation Trick

A simple but underused technique is asking the AI to continue. If the output stopped early, the next prompt can be continue from where you stopped or expand the previous response with more detail in section three. The AI generally picks up where it left off and produces additional content. This works particularly well for long outputs that exceed a single response in length.

9.3 Reducing Hallucination Like Responses

AI models sometimes produce outputs that contain inaccurate information, fabricated quotes, invented statistics, or references to sources that do not exist. This phenomenon is often called hallucination. Hallucination is one of the most serious failure modes because the output looks confident and authoritative even when it is wrong.

Why Hallucinations Occur

AI models are trained to produce plausible text. When they do not have specific information, they fill the gap with the kind of text that would be likely to appear in their training data. This pattern matching is what makes them powerful. It is also what makes them prone to fabrication when stretched beyond what they actually know. The AI is not lying. It is generating what it believes a likely answer would look like.

Tasks that ask for specific facts, recent events, named sources, or precise numbers are particularly prone to hallucination. The AI may produce a confident sounding statistic or a plausible looking citation that does not exist. This is dangerous in any context where the output will be used as a foundation for decisions or shared with others as accurate.

How to Reduce Hallucination

Several techniques reduce hallucination. The first is to provide source material explicitly. If you want the AI to write about a specific topic, paste in the source material and ask the AI to draw only from what is provided. The instruction use only the information in the source material above is one of the most powerful guards against fabrication.

The second technique is to ask the AI to flag uncertainty. Phrases like if you are not sure of a fact, say so explicitly invite the AI to admit gaps rather than fill them. The AI's training rewards confident answers, so this prompt level instruction is often necessary to surface uncertainty.

The third technique is to ask for verifiable specifics rather than vague claims. Instead of asking for arguments in favor of a position, ask for arguments along with the empirical evidence or sources that would support each. The AI is more careful when it must point to evidence than when it can make general claims.

The fourth technique is to verify externally for any high stakes claim. AI output is a starting point, not an authority. For anything that will be published, presented, or used as the basis of a decision, verify the specific claims through trusted sources. This is not a failure of the AI. It is responsible practice.

Hallucination Resistant Prompt Patterns

Pattern	Example Phrasing	How It Helps
Source bound	Use only the information in the document above.	Removes the AI's need to invent.
Uncertainty flag	If unsure, say so. Do not guess.	Invites the AI to surface gaps.
Evidence required	For each claim, cite the source from the input.	Forces grounding in real material.
No invention	Do not invent names, dates, or statistics.	Explicit prohibition on fabrication.
Cross check	List your assumptions. We will verify them.	Surfaces what the AI is taking for granted.

Hallucination Warning

AI output that mentions specific names, dates, statistics, quotes, or citations should always be verified before being published or used in decision making. Treat the AI as a brilliant assistant who occasionally misremembers details. Trust but verify.

9.4 Consistency in Repeated Prompts

If you run the same prompt twice, you may not get the same output. AI models include some randomness in their generation, which means responses vary across attempts. This is a feature in some contexts, like brainstorming where you want diverse ideas, and a problem in others, like data extraction where you want reliable consistent output.

Why Output Varies

Output variation comes from two sources. The first is the AI's internal randomness, sometimes called sampling temperature, which determines how much variability the AI introduces in its choices. The second is the inherent ambiguity in the prompt itself. Vague prompts produce more varied output because the AI has more interpretive leeway. Tight prompts produce more consistent output because the interpretive space is smaller.

How to Improve Consistency

To improve consistency without sacrificing quality, do four things. First, tighten the prompt itself. Eliminate ambiguity. Specify format, length, tone, and structure precisely. Second, use few shot examples to lock in the desired pattern. Examples are remarkably effective at producing consistent output across attempts. Third, ask for structured output, like JSON or labeled sections, which constrains the AI more than freeform prose. Fourth, when possible, use lower randomness settings if your tool supports them. Lower temperature produces more deterministic output, though at some cost to creativity.

Consistency is not always desirable. For brainstorming, exploration, and creative work, variation is the point. The skill is matching the level of consistency to the task. Tight when you need reliability. Loose when you need range.

9.5 Do's and Don'ts of Prompt Writing

To close this chapter, here is a consolidated list of working habits that experienced prompt writers consistently follow. Treat these as a quick reference.

Do's

- Do start with a clear action verb. The first word of your prompt sets the kind of work you are asking for.
- Do specify your audience. Different audiences need different language, depth, and examples.
- Do specify the format. List, paragraph, table, or JSON, the format influences both presentation and underlying reasoning.
- Do specify length. Words, sentences, paragraphs, or sections, give the AI a target.
- Do provide context the AI needs. Personal, audience, situational, reference, or stylistic context all help.
- Do use examples for unusual tasks. Few shot prompts teach the AI custom patterns more efficiently than verbal description.

- Do iterate. The first attempt is rarely the best. Refine based on what the output reveals.
- Do break complex work into steps. Multi step or chained prompts produce higher quality output for non trivial tasks.
- Do verify high stakes claims. AI output is a starting point, not an authority on factual matters.
- Do save your best prompts. Effective prompts are reusable assets. Treat them like saved templates.

Don'ts

- Do not be vague when you can be specific. Vagueness is the most common cause of disappointing output.
- Do not stack many requests in one prompt. The AI rations attention across multiple asks.
- Do not assume the AI knows you. Provide context rather than relying on history.
- Do not rely only on negative instructions. Positive guidance produces better results than don't lists.
- Do not give up after one try. Most successful prompts come from multiple iterations.
- Do not blindly trust factual claims. Verify before publishing or deciding.
- Do not over constrain creative work. Specify what matters, leave room for surprise on the rest.
- Do not use jargon the AI may not recognize without defining it.
- Do not forget to specify tone. Default voice rarely fits a specific use case perfectly.
- Do not overload examples. Three to five well chosen examples are usually enough.

The Single Most Important Habit

More than any other do or don't, the single most important habit is reading the output critically and asking what specifically would need to change in the prompt to produce a better one. That diagnostic loop, repeated, is how prompt writing skill compounds over time.

9.6 Chapter Recap

This chapter covered troubleshooting and the working habits of effective prompt writers.

- Irrelevant outputs usually trace back to vagueness, mixed requests, or missing context. Sharpen, separate, or supply.

- Incomplete answers come from unclear scope, length boundaries, or too many requests. Specify scope, ask for continuation, or break the task apart.
- Hallucination occurs when the AI fills gaps with plausible but invented content. Bound to source material, ask for uncertainty, and verify high stakes claims.
- Consistency varies across attempts due to model randomness and prompt ambiguity. Tighten, use examples, and prefer structured outputs when consistency matters.
- The do's and don'ts list captures the working habits of effective prompt writers. Reading the output critically is the single most important habit.

Practice Exercise

Most prompt problems are tractable when approached systematically. This exercise walks you through the systematic diagnosis.

1. Pick a prompt that has been giving you trouble. Choose a real one, not a synthetic example.
2. Diagnose the failure mode. Is the output irrelevant, incomplete, hallucinated, or inconsistent across attempts?
3. Match the diagnosis to its corresponding fix from this chapter. Each failure mode has its own playbook.
4. Apply the fix and rewrite the prompt accordingly.
5. Rerun the prompt and verify whether the fix produced the improvement you expected.
6. If the original problem persists, repeat the diagnosis. There may be a second underlying cause.

Notice how often the fix is straightforward once the diagnosis is clear. The diagnostic vocabulary is what unlocks the fixes.

9.7 Diagnosing AI Output Problems Systematically

Section 9.1 introduced fixing irrelevant outputs. This expansion provides a systematic diagnostic framework that you can apply to any AI output that disappoints. The framework asks five questions in order. Each question, if answered yes, points to a specific repair.

Question 1: Did the AI Produce What Was Asked?

Read the output carefully and ask whether it actually addresses the task in the prompt. If the AI wrote a paragraph when you asked for a list, or summarized when you asked for analysis, the issue is at the level of basic comprehension. The repair is to make the action verb more prominent and to restate the task at the end of the prompt as a summary instruction.

Question 2: Did the AI Address the Right Topic?

If the AI did the right kind of work but on a slightly different topic, the issue is topic drift. Maybe the prompt's topic was ambiguous and the AI picked a related but different topic. The repair is to make the topic explicit and to add framing that prevents drift, like the topic is X, not Y, even if Y comes up.

Question 3: Did the AI Use the Right Information?

If the AI used facts, references, or context that does not match what you provided, the issue is information sourcing. Maybe the AI invented information rather than drawing from your source material. The repair is to bound the AI to your source explicitly: use only the information in the source material below.

Question 4: Did the AI Apply the Right Constraints?

If the AI ignored your length, format, tone, or other constraints, the issue is constraint compliance. Constraints sometimes get lost in long prompts or fail to be salient enough. The repair is to restate critical constraints near the end of the prompt and to phrase them as must rather than should.

Question 5: Did the AI Produce Output That Lands?

Even when the substance is right and the constraints are followed, output sometimes feels off. The voice is wrong. The emphasis is misplaced. The reader experience is dampened. The issue is craft. The repair is more elusive: examples of voice, more specific tonal guidance, or asking the AI to critique and revise its own draft.

The Five Question Diagnostic

Run through these five questions in order whenever output disappoints. The first question that gets a no points to where the issue lives. Repair is targeted from there. This systematic approach beats vague rewriting every time.

9.8 Hallucination: Practical Defenses

Section 9.3 introduced hallucination. This expansion goes deeper into practical defenses, with attention to the kinds of tasks most prone to hallucination and the prompt patterns that reduce it most effectively.

Tasks Most Prone to Hallucination

Hallucination is more likely when the task involves any of the following.

- Specific names of people, places, or organizations. The AI may produce plausible sounding names that do not exist.
- Specific dates, numbers, or statistics. The AI may invent figures that fit the context but are not real.
- Specific quotes or citations. The AI may fabricate quotes or cite sources that do not exist.
- Recent events. The AI may invent details about events that occurred near or after its training cutoff.
- Niche topics. The AI may fill gaps in coverage of specialized subjects with plausible but wrong information.
- Code involving specific libraries. The AI may invent functions or methods that do not exist in the actual library.
- Legal or regulatory specifics. The AI may invent statutes, court cases, or regulations that sound plausible.
- Medical or scientific specifics. The AI may produce confident but inaccurate technical details.

Whenever your task touches one of these categories, hallucination defense should be active. The patterns below help.

The Source Bound Pattern

```
Use only the information in the source material below. Do not invent facts,
names, or numbers. If a question cannot be answered from the source, say so
explicitly rather than guessing.  [Source material] ...
```

This pattern dramatically reduces hallucination on tasks where the source material is comprehensive enough to support the work. It also makes hallucination easier to spot, since any output that goes beyond the source is now visibly out of bounds.

The Uncertainty Flag Pattern

```
After producing the response, list any specific claims you are not fully
confident about, with the reason for each uncertainty. Do not flag general
points, only specific facts, numbers, or names.
```

This pattern invites the AI to surface uncertainty rather than hide it. It produces output that is both useful and honest about its limits, which is often more valuable than confidently stated content of unknown reliability.

The Reasoning Required Pattern

```
For each claim in your response, briefly explain how you arrived at it: which
source it came from, what reasoning it depends on, or whether it is general
knowledge.
```

This pattern forces the AI to articulate the basis for its claims. Claims with no clear basis become visible. The user can then probe the suspicious claims further or replace them with verified information.

The Verify Externally Habit

Beyond prompt patterns, the most important defense is the habit of external verification. For any AI output that includes specific names, dates, statistics, or quotes, treat the output as a starting point and verify the specifics through trusted sources before publishing or relying on them. The AI does the heavy lifting of structure and language. You do the final fact check. The combination produces work that is both efficient and accurate.

9.9 Consistency: When and How to Achieve It

Section 9.4 covered consistency. This expansion looks at when consistency matters most, when variation matters more, and how to dial in the right level for each task.

When Consistency Matters

Consistency matters most for production pipelines, structured data extraction, classification tasks, customer facing communications that follow brand standards, and any task where the same input should always produce roughly the same output. In these contexts, variation is noise that degrades reliability.

When Variation Matters

Variation matters most for brainstorming, creative work, ideation, exploration, and any task where multiple distinct outputs are the point. Asking an AI to generate ten taglines should produce ten different taglines, not ten variations of the same tagline. Variation is the value.

Achieving High Consistency

Several techniques together produce high consistency.

1. Tighten the prompt. Eliminate ambiguity. Specify format, length, and structure precisely.
2. Use few shot examples. Three to five examples lock in a pattern far more reliably than verbal description.
3. Specify structured output. JSON or labeled sections constrain the AI more than freeform prose.

4. Lower the randomness setting. If your tool exposes a temperature parameter, lower values produce more deterministic output.
5. Use the same model and same prompt formulation across uses. Even small changes in either can shift the output distribution.

Achieving High Variation

Several techniques together produce high variation.

1. Loosen the prompt. Allow the AI to interpret the task in different ways.
2. Ask for many candidates at once. Generate twenty options produces more diverse output than running one prompt twenty times.
3. Specify the diversity explicitly. Each option should approach the task from a noticeably different angle invites the AI to spread out.
4. Raise the randomness setting if available. Higher temperature produces more varied output.
5. Vary the prompt formulation across runs. Slight changes in framing produce noticeably different outputs.

9.10 Twenty Five Working Tips

Beyond the do's and don'ts in section 9.5, here are twenty five working tips that experienced prompt writers rely on regularly.

1. Read the prompt aloud before sending. Awkward phrasing often reveals issues your eyes glide over.
2. Specify the output format every time. Even when you think the format is obvious, it is not always obvious to the AI.
3. Use specific numbers rather than vague descriptors. Five reasons beats several reasons every time.
4. Put critical instructions both at the start and end of the prompt. Double anchoring improves compliance.
5. Use clear delimiters around source material. Triple dashes, XML tags, or labeled sections prevent the AI from confusing input with instructions.
6. State assumptions explicitly. Phrases like assume the reader is technical or assume the budget is unlimited remove guesswork.
7. Specify the level of detail. The depth of analysis matters as much as the topic.

8. Ask for what you want, not what you do not want. Positive guidance outperforms negative guidance most of the time.
9. Provide an example or two when the task is unusual. Examples teach more efficiently than description.
10. Iterate deliberately. Each refinement should target a specific issue, not vaguely improve the prompt.
11. Save prompts that work. Building a personal library compounds over time.
12. Use the same vocabulary the AI uses. Domain specific words from the AI's earlier responses are usually well tuned for the conversation.
13. When in doubt, add structure. Labeled sections, lists, or tables make output more usable than freeform prose.
14. Reset the conversation when it goes sideways. Sometimes a fresh start is faster than recovery.
15. Use the AI to improve your prompts. Ask it to suggest improvements to a prompt you have drafted.
16. Verify factual claims independently. AI is a starting point, not a source.
17. Vary your few shot examples for diversity. Edge cases and central cases together produce robust output.
18. Use roles for any task that benefits from a perspective. Roles are an underused leverage point.
19. Specify length in multiple units. 200 words or roughly three paragraphs is more reliable than either alone.
20. Be explicit about the audience. Different audiences require different language and depth.
21. Use templates for tasks you do repeatedly. Each repetition gets faster and more reliable.
22. Tag your saved prompts. Tags make finding the right prompt faster than scrolling.
23. Document why each saved prompt works. Future you will thank present you.
24. Share what works with your team. Team libraries grow faster than personal ones.
25. Stay curious. The best prompt writers never stop learning new techniques.

9.11 Recovery Patterns When Things Go Wrong

Sometimes a conversation goes off the rails. The AI keeps producing output that does not match what you want. Each iteration seems to make things slightly worse rather than better. Recovery is possible, but the right approach depends on the failure mode.

Recovery Pattern 1: The Fresh Start

If the conversation has accumulated context that is now confusing the AI, start a fresh conversation. Write a clean prompt that includes only what is needed. The fresh start often produces better output in one shot than ten more iterations on the troubled thread.

Recovery Pattern 2: The Explicit Reset

Within a conversation, sometimes you can reset by being very explicit. Forget what we discussed. Here is a fresh request, treated independently. Then provide the new prompt. The AI usually respects this reset and produces fresh output without bringing in the troubled context.

Recovery Pattern 3: The Critique and Pivot

Sometimes the issue is not the conversation but the approach. Ask the AI to critique its own recent output. The critique often surfaces the issue in a way that helps you write a better next prompt. Pivot based on what the critique reveals.

Recovery Pattern 4: The Smaller Task

If a complex task is producing tangled output, break it into smaller pieces. Run a smaller task. Get a clean output. Then run another smaller task with the first output as input. The chain of small tasks often succeeds where the single big task struggled.

Recovery Pattern 5: The Different Model

If your tool exposes multiple AI models, sometimes switching models produces dramatically different output. A model that struggles with your task may have a sibling that handles it well. Experimentation across models is a small but real lever.

> **When in Doubt, Reset**
>
> Recovery is sometimes faster than refinement. The fresh start is underused. If a conversation feels stuck, try a fresh prompt with a fresh framing. The improvement is often dramatic.

9.12 Building Resilience into Your Prompting Practice

Beyond troubleshooting individual prompts, there is value in building resilience into your overall prompting practice. Resilient practice means that when things go wrong, you have systems and habits that help you recover quickly. Below are several elements of a resilient practice.

Backup Templates

For any high stakes task you do regularly, keep a backup template. If your usual prompt produces unexpected output one day, the backup can be tried instantly. The backup might use a different design pattern, different examples, or different constraints. Diversity in your library produces resilience under stress.

Validation Steps

For tasks where the output will be used in important contexts, build a validation step into your workflow. After the AI produces the output, you read it carefully against a checklist. Did it cover all required elements? Did it follow the format? Did it match the tone? The validation catches issues before they propagate.

Documentation Habits

When you find a prompt that works well, document not just the prompt but the context. What kind of task is it for? What audience? What were the alternatives you tried? This documentation helps future you remember not just the prompt but the reasoning behind it.

Periodic Library Review

Once a quarter, review your prompt library. Are there prompts that no longer match your needs? Templates that have been replaced by better versions? Prompts that have stopped producing the output you wanted because the underlying task has shifted? Pruning the library keeps it sharp.

Continuous Learning

The prompting field is still evolving. New techniques appear. Models change. What worked last year may not be optimal today. Reading, experimenting, and updating your practice keeps you growing rather than stagnating. Resilient practitioners stay curious.

> *Resilient prompting is less about avoiding problems and more about recovering from them quickly. Build the systems that help you bounce back, and prompting becomes a much more reliable part of your work.*

9.13 Comprehensive Failure Mode Catalog

Below is a comprehensive catalog of AI output failure modes, organized by category, with the prompt level repair for each. Use this as a diagnostic reference when output disappoints.

Substance Failures

Failure	Repair
Generic when specifics needed	Add detailed context about your specific situation
Specific when overview needed	Specify the level of abstraction explicitly
Off topic	Sharpen the topic boundary, add what is in scope and out of scope
Contains invented facts	Bind to source material, ask for uncertainty flags
Misses your actual question	Restate the question explicitly at end of prompt
Avoids taking a position	Ask for a recommendation, not just analysis
Hedges excessively	Specify the level of confidence you want
Confident but inaccurate	Verify externally, ask AI to point to evidence
Repeats itself across paragraphs	Specify that each section should make a distinct point
Misses key implications	Ask explicitly for second order effects

Structure Failures

Failure	Repair
Wrong format	Specify format explicitly
Sections imbalanced	Specify size per section
No clear organization	Specify section labels and order
List when paragraph wanted	State paragraph format explicitly
Paragraph when list wanted	State list format and bullet count

Failure	Repair
Headers missing	Require labeled sections
Bullets too long	Specify one sentence per bullet
Bullets too short	Specify complete sentences per bullet
Missing required sections	List required sections explicitly
Extra sections you did not want	Specify exactly which sections, and that no others should appear

Style Failures

Failure	Repair
Too formal	Specify casual or warm tone
Too informal	Specify professional tone
Voice does not match brand	Provide voice examples
Too jargon heavy	Specify non technical audience
Too simple	Specify expert audience
Inconsistent tone across sections	Specify tone explicitly and at multiple points in prompt
Tone does not fit task	Pair tonal descriptors for nuance
Too sales pitchy	Forbid marketing language explicitly
Too apologetic	Specify confident tone
Too detached	Specify warm tone

Scale Failures

Failure	Repair
Too long	Specify maximum length
Too short	Specify minimum or expected length
Padded	Forbid restating, summarizing, or generic transitions
Truncated	Break into multiple prompts, ask for continuation
Wandered off topic by end	Restate scope and topic at end of prompt
Detail uneven across topics	Specify same depth for each subtopic
Lacks the depth you wanted	Ask for second level deep, with example, evidence, and counterargument per main point
More depth than you wanted	Specify high level overview, no more than X words per section

The Diagnostic Habit

Build the habit of looking up the failure category before rewriting. Most AI output issues fall into one of these categories. The repair is targeted. The next attempt is much closer to what you wanted. The minute spent diagnosing saves the five minutes of vague rewriting.

9.14 Stuck Conversations: Patterns and Recoveries

Sometimes conversations with AI get stuck. The output stops improving despite iteration. Below are common stuck patterns and the recoveries that work.

Pattern: The Same Mistake Recurs

Symptom: You correct an issue, the AI fixes it that turn, but the issue returns in the next response. Cause: the underlying prompt has not changed, only the latest correction has. The AI returns to its default in the next round.

Recovery: Bake the correction into the prompt itself, not just into one round of conversation. If you keep saying make it shorter, set the length explicitly in the next prompt rather than continuing to ask for shortening.

Pattern: The Drift in Quality

Symptom: Early responses are excellent, but later in the conversation the output becomes less focused, less accurate, or less aligned with the original task.

Recovery: Restate the task and the standards. Long conversations accumulate context that may be confusing the AI. A clear restatement of what you want, written as if starting fresh, often resets the focus.

Pattern: The Compounding Errors

Symptom: An error in an early response gets carried forward, and subsequent responses build on the error rather than correcting it.

Recovery: Reset the conversation. Fresh start with a corrected baseline. Sometimes the only way out of compounding errors is to start over.

Pattern: The Surface Improvement

Symptom: Each iteration produces visible changes, but the underlying issue remains. The AI is making cosmetic adjustments rather than addressing the real problem.

Recovery: Diagnose more precisely. Ask the AI to explain what it changed and why. Sometimes the AI's explanation reveals that you and it are not aligned on what the issue is. Aligning on the issue often resolves the cycle.

Pattern: The Loop

Symptom: You ask for a change. The AI makes it. You realize the new version has a problem the old one did not. You ask for the old behavior back. The AI restores it. Now the original issue returns. You are oscillating between two flawed versions.

Recovery: Combine both desired qualities in a single prompt. The earlier version was better at X but worse at Y. Produce a version that maintains X and addresses Y. The AI can often integrate when you spell out both targets simultaneously.

9.15 The Self Reflective Prompter

The most advanced prompt writers do something most beginners do not: they reflect on their own prompts and conversations as data. They notice patterns in what works and what does not. They learn from their own mistakes. They build a personal practice that improves over time, almost without effort, because they pay attention.

The Practice of Reflection

Reflection does not require formal journaling, though that helps for some people. It can be a few minutes at the end of each day, looking back at the prompts you sent. Which produced excellent output? What did they have in common? Which produced disappointing output? What was missing? The patterns emerge over weeks.

Reflection Questions

1. Which prompts in the last week produced output I was genuinely proud to use?
2. What did those prompts have in common, beyond the obvious differences in topic?
3. Which prompts produced output I had to extensively rewrite?
4. In hindsight, what was missing from those prompts?
5. What is one habit I want to build in my prompting next week?

The Compounding Effect

Self reflection is the engine of improvement that compounds across years. Most prompt writers stop improving once they reach an acceptable level. The reflective ones keep improving long after that. Over time, the gap between reflective and non reflective prompters becomes large. Reflection is the small habit that makes that gap.

> *The prompter who reflects on their own practice is the prompter whose practice keeps growing. The prompter who only practices, without reflection, plateaus at whatever level happens to feel acceptable.*

Chapter 10: Building Reusable Prompt Systems

We have arrived at the final chapter. Up to this point, the book has focused on individual prompts, how to design them, structure them, optimize them, and troubleshoot them. In this chapter, we step back and look at the bigger picture. How do you move from writing one prompt at a time to building systems of prompts that can be reused, shared, and scaled across your work? This is where prompt engineering crosses from craft into infrastructure.

Reusable prompt systems matter because most of the prompts you write are not unique. You write similar prompts for similar tasks again and again. Without a system, each prompt is reinvented from scratch. With a system, common tasks become predictable and fast, and rare tasks build on a strong foundation rather than starting from a blank page. This chapter teaches the basics of designing, organizing, and scaling such systems.

10.1 Creating Prompt Templates

The simplest building block of a reusable system is the prompt template. A template is a prompt with placeholders where the variable parts go. The fixed parts capture what does not change from one use to the next. The placeholders mark what does. Templates turn one off prompts into reusable patterns.

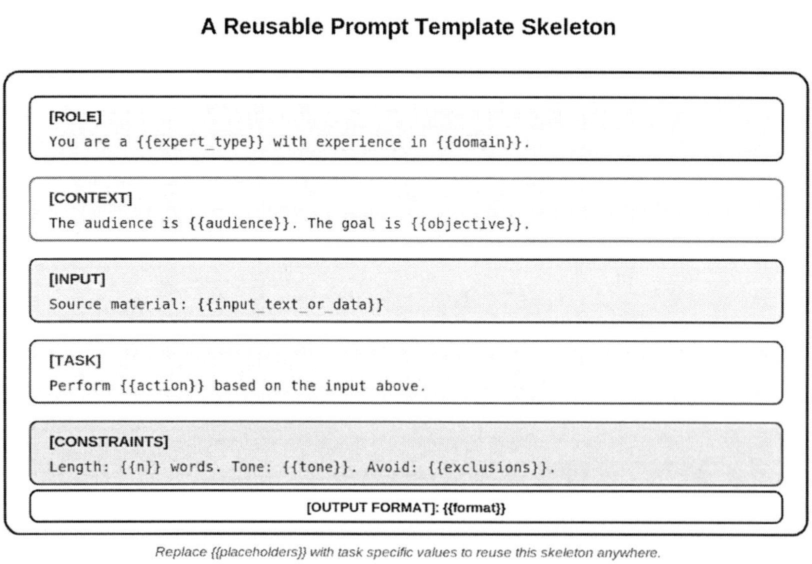

Figure 10.1: A simple reusable prompt template skeleton.

Anatomy of a Template

A useful template typically has five labeled regions, each holding a specific kind of information. Role at the top sets the AI's perspective. Context describes the audience and situation. Input holds the source material the AI should use. Task names the action the AI should perform. Constraints capture length, tone, format, and any other rules. Each region can include placeholders, marked in a recognizable way like double curly braces, that get filled in for each use.

```
[ROLE] You are a {{expert_type}} with deep experience in {{domain}}.  [CONTEXT]
The audience is {{audience}}. The goal is {{objective}}.  [INPUT] Source
material: {{input_text}}  [TASK] Perform {{action}} based on the input above.
[CONSTRAINTS] Length: {{length}}. Tone: {{tone}}. Avoid: {{exclusions}}.
[OUTPUT FORMAT] {{format}}
```

Notice the structure. The fixed scaffolding is recognizable. The placeholders are clearly marked. To use the template, you fill in the placeholders with your specific values for the current task. The result is a complete, well structured prompt produced in seconds rather than minutes.

Designing Good Placeholders

The art of template design is choosing the right placeholders. Too few placeholders and the template is rigid, useful for only a narrow range of tasks. Too many and the template is bloated, requiring you to fill in fields you do not always need. The best templates have placeholders that capture genuine variability and let everything else stay fixed.

A useful exercise is to write five real prompts you would actually send for the same kind of task, then look at what differs across the five. The things that differ are good candidates for placeholders. The things that stay the same are good candidates for fixed text. This exercise produces templates that fit your real workflow rather than abstract prompt theory.

10.2 Designing Prompt Frameworks for Repeated Use

A framework is a step beyond a template. While a template is a single fillable prompt, a framework is a structured approach to a class of tasks, often combining multiple templates, decision rules, and best practices into a coherent system. Frameworks scale beyond individual prompts to entire workflows.

Examples of Useful Frameworks

Some frameworks have become widely known in the prompt engineering community because they capture useful patterns in a memorable way. Each framework gives you a checklist of elements to include in the prompt for a particular kind of task.

Framework	Components	Best For
Role, Action, Format	Who the AI is, what it should do, how the output should look	Quick prompts where minimal structure helps
Context, Instruction, Examples, Output	Background, task, few shot examples, expected format	Custom or unusual tasks needing examples
Persona, Task, Constraints, Format	Role, action, rules, structure	Professional content with clear standards
Goal, Audience, Tone, Length, Format	What the output should achieve, for whom, in what voice, how long, in what shape	Marketing, communications, audience facing work
Input, Steps, Output	Source material, a sequence of operations, target format	Data extraction, transformation, multi step processing

These named frameworks are not magic. They are mnemonics. The reason to learn them is that having a memorable acronym helps you remember to include the elements that make prompts strong. The elements themselves, role, audience, format, examples, constraints, are all things we have covered in earlier chapters. Frameworks just package them for fast recall.

Building Your Own Framework

Over time, you will likely develop your own framework that fits the kinds of tasks you do most often. The process is straightforward. Look at the prompts you write most frequently. Identify the components that consistently appear in your strong prompts. Name those components in a way that is easy for you to remember. Use the name as a checklist whenever you sit down to write a prompt for that kind of task. Personal frameworks, tuned to your real work, are often more useful than generic ones because they fit your context exactly.

10.3 Structuring Prompts for Different Tasks

Different kinds of tasks benefit from different prompt structures. A summarization task and a creative writing task may share the same building blocks but use them in different proportions. Knowing which structures fit which tasks helps you reach for the right shape quickly.

Common Task Categories and Their Prompt Structures

Below is a survey of common task categories and the prompt structures that suit them. Treat these as starting points, not strict rules. Each can be adapted to your specific situation.

Summarization Tasks

Summarization prompts work best with three core elements. The instruction with explicit length, the source material, and the audience or purpose. The structure looks like, summarize the document below in 150 words or fewer for a busy executive who wants to know whether the project is on track.

Analysis Tasks

Analysis prompts work best with role assignment, the source material, the analytical lens, and the output structure. Acting as a financial analyst, review the data below and identify the three most significant trends. Present each trend in a labeled section with a one paragraph explanation. The role and lens together produce focused, professional analysis.

Generation Tasks

Generation prompts, where the AI is creating something from scratch, benefit from clear instruction, audience, tone, length, and format constraints. Generate a 200 word product description for a wireless headphone. The audience is health conscious millennials. Use a casual, energetic tone. Format as one short opening paragraph followed by three feature highlights. The richer the constraints, the more aligned the output.

Transformation Tasks

Transformation prompts move content from one form to another. They work best with the source material, the desired output form, and the rules of transformation. Convert the bulleted notes below into a flowing two paragraph executive summary. Preserve all decisions and action items, but smooth out the language and remove repetition.

Decision Support Tasks

Decision support prompts ask the AI to help you choose. They work best with the context, the options, the criteria, and the output format. Compare these three project management tools across five criteria: cost, ease of use, integrations, scalability, and support quality. Format as a table, then close with a single recommendation paragraph that names the best fit for a 15 person consulting firm.

Creative Tasks

Creative prompts benefit from looser structure with strategic constraints. Specify enough to direct the work but leave room for surprise. Write a 400 word short story about a librarian who discovers a hidden room. The tone should be warm and slightly mysterious. End with a question rather than a resolution. The constraints set the stage. The AI fills it.

10.4 Organizing Prompt Libraries

Once you have many useful prompts and templates, the question becomes how to organize them. A disorganized collection of files is almost as useless as no collection at all. The goal is to make it fast and easy to find the right prompt for the moment, and to keep the collection improving over time.

Principles of a Useful Prompt Library

Several principles distinguish a useful library from an unused one. A useful library is searchable. You can find prompts by keyword, category, or tag without scrolling through everything. A useful library is categorized. Prompts are grouped in ways that match how you think about your work. A useful library has metadata. Each prompt is labeled with what it does, when to use it, and any caveats. A useful library is curated. Old or replaced prompts are pruned, not just accumulated. A useful library evolves. As you find better versions of common prompts, the library is updated to reflect what you have learned.

Categorization Strategies

There are several ways to categorize prompts, and the right scheme depends on how you work.

1. By task category. Summarization, analysis, generation, transformation, decision support, creative.
2. By domain. Marketing, engineering, finance, legal, customer support, research.
3. By output format. Reports, emails, code, lists, tables, slides, scripts.
4. By workflow stage. Brainstorming, drafting, editing, reviewing, finalizing.
5. By complexity. Quick prompts, multi step prompts, prompt chains.

Most working libraries combine two or three of these schemes through tags. A single prompt might be tagged as analysis, marketing, and report at the same time. The combination makes it findable through any of the three categories.

Documentation Each Prompt

For each prompt or template in your library, three pieces of metadata are particularly valuable. The name should describe what the prompt does in a few words. The use case should describe when this prompt is the right choice. The notes should capture anything you have learned about its strengths, weaknesses, or variations. Without this metadata, prompts age quickly. With it, they remain useful for as long as the underlying tasks remain relevant.

> **Library Versioning**
>
> Treat your prompt library like code. When you find a better version of a prompt, save the new version alongside the old one rather than overwriting. You may want to refer back. You may also want to compare which version produces better output across different kinds of inputs.

10.5 Scaling Prompt Usage in Daily Workflows

The final question is how to integrate prompts into your daily working life so that they become second nature rather than special occasions. Scaling here does not mean enterprise scale. It means the everyday scale of an individual whose work benefits from regularly using AI thoughtfully.

Habits That Scale Prompting

Several habits, once established, dramatically expand the value you get from AI.

1. Save what works. When a prompt produces excellent output, save it before moving on. The temptation to skip this step is strong. Resist it. Saving takes seconds and pays dividends for months.
2. Build templates from your best prompts. Once you have used a prompt successfully a few times, turn it into a template by adding placeholders. The template can then serve dozens of similar future tasks.
3. Use AI to write prompts. The AI can help you write better prompts. Ask it to suggest improvements to a prompt you have drafted, or to generate a few variations for a task you are working on.
4. Review your library periodically. Once a quarter, scan your library for prompts that are no longer useful or that have been replaced by better versions. Prune. The library stays sharp.
5. Share with your team. If you work with others, share your best prompts and templates. Different perspectives often produce improvements. A team library grows faster than an individual one.
6. Stay curious. The field of prompting is still young, and new techniques continue to emerge. Read, experiment, and keep your library evolving.

Building Your Personal Prompt System

If you take only one practice from this chapter, let it be this. Start a prompt library today, even if it begins with just three or four prompts. Add to it consistently. Refine over time. Within months you will have a system that makes routine work faster and complex work more reliable. Within a year you will wonder how you ever worked without it.

The library does not have to be elaborate. A simple text document with named sections works. A note taking app with tagged notes works. A spreadsheet with columns for name, category, prompt, and notes works. The tool matters less than the habit. The habit is the thing that compounds.

10.6 Closing Thoughts: Becoming a Better Communicator

We have come a long way together in this book. We started with the most basic question, what is a prompt, and we have ended with the design of reusable systems that can scale across teams and workflows. The journey has covered foundations, structure, patterns, techniques, optimization, troubleshooting, and frameworks. Along the way, examples, exercises, and analogies have grounded each idea in concrete practice.

Take a moment to reflect on what has changed for you between the first page and this one. The vocabulary you now have for thinking about prompts. The patterns you can now reach for. The mistakes you can now identify in your own writing. The discipline of structure, context, constraints, and output expectation. These are not just techniques. They are habits of mind. And once they are yours, they belong to you in every interaction with AI you will ever have.

Prompting Is Communication

There is a deeper lesson hidden inside everything we have covered. Prompting is communication. Every principle that makes a great prompt, clarity, specificity, audience awareness, structured thinking, also makes great communication with humans. The skills overlap completely. What makes a great prompt makes a great brief. What makes a great brief makes a great instruction. What makes a great instruction makes a great teacher, manager, mentor, and collaborator.

In this sense, learning to prompt well is not just a technical skill. It is an exercise in becoming a clearer thinker and a better communicator. The careful word choice that gets the AI to do what you want is the same careful word choice that gets a colleague, a partner, or a child to understand what you mean. The discipline of separating intent from instruction from context is a discipline that improves every conversation you have.

The Craft Continues

AI tools will continue to evolve. New models, new interfaces, new capabilities will emerge. Some of the specific techniques in this book may shift as those changes unfold. But the underlying principles, clarity, structure, audience awareness, iteration, the four building blocks, the design patterns, the troubleshooting habits, will remain. The craft of prompting is a craft of communication, and communication is one of the oldest and deepest skills humans have. The tools change. The craft endures.

> *The best prompt writers are not the ones who know the most tricks. They are the ones who think clearly about what they want, communicate it precisely, and iterate when reality disagrees with their first guess.*

Where to Go From Here

Five suggestions to keep your skills growing after you close this book.

1. Use what you have learned. Tomorrow, write at least one prompt that uses all four building blocks. The day after, do it again. Practice converts knowledge into skill.
2. Build your library. Save your best prompts. Tag them. Refine them. Within months you will have an asset that compounds in value over time.
3. Read other people's prompts. There are growing communities and resources where people share what works for them. New ideas come from exposure to other styles and contexts.
4. Teach what you know. Explaining a concept to someone else is one of the fastest ways to deepen your own understanding. Find someone earlier in their journey and share what you have learned.
5. Stay humble. Even after years of practice, every new task can teach you something. The moment you think you have mastered prompting is the moment you stop learning. Keep the beginner's mind.

A Final Note

Thank you for reading this book. You started as someone curious about prompts. You finish as someone equipped to design them with intention. What you do with that capability is up to you. Whatever you build, whatever you write, whatever you create with these tools, may you do it thoughtfully, carefully, and with the kindness toward your AI collaborators that they would extend to you if they could.

10.7 Chapter and Book Recap

This final chapter wrapped up the book with the architecture of reusable prompt systems.

- Templates capture fixed and variable parts of prompts you use repeatedly, turning one off prompts into reusable patterns.
- Frameworks add structure beyond individual templates, packaging best practices into memorable patterns for entire classes of tasks.
- Different task categories benefit from different prompt structures. Summarization, analysis, generation, transformation, decision support, and creative tasks each have their own conventions.
- A useful prompt library is searchable, categorized, documented, curated, and evolves over time.
- Habits that scale prompting include saving what works, building templates from successes, using AI to refine prompts, periodic library reviews, team sharing, and continued learning.
- Prompting is communication. The skills that make a great prompt are the skills that make a great communicator with humans.

A Final Practice Exercise

Begin building your personal prompt library this week. The steps below take less than an hour to complete and lay the foundation for a system that will pay back across years.

1. Pick at least three prompts that have produced excellent output for you in real work.
2. For each prompt, write a one line description of what it does and when to use it.
3. Save them somewhere durable. A notes app, a document, or a spreadsheet all work. The tool matters less than the habit.
4. Add to the library every time you find a prompt worth keeping. Resist the temptation to skip this step under deadline pressure.
5. Once a month, review the library. Prune what no longer applies. Refine prompts that have better versions now.

Within a month, you will have a working system. Within a year, you will have an asset that quietly improves nearly every piece of work you do with AI. The journey through this book ends here. The practice begins now.

10.8 The Template Design Process

Section 10.1 introduced templates. This expansion walks through the deliberate process of designing a high quality template, step by step, with examples.

Step 1: Identify a Repeated Task

Templates are valuable for tasks you do repeatedly. Identifying the repeats is the first step. Look at the prompts you have written in the last month. Group them by similarity. The groups with three or more similar prompts are template candidates. The more often you do a task, the more leverage a template provides.

Step 2: Identify the Variable Parts

Within each group of similar prompts, examine what changes between instances. The audience may change. The source material may change. The desired length may vary. The tone may shift. The things that change are the variable parts. The things that stay the same are the fixed parts. The variable parts become placeholders in the template.

Step 3: Write the Skeleton

Write the prompt with placeholders where the variable parts go. Use a recognizable placeholder syntax, like double curly braces or all caps in brackets. The skeleton should read as a coherent prompt with the placeholders making sense in context.

Step 4: Test on Real Tasks

Use the template on three or four real tasks you would normally do. Notice where it works and where it does not. Maybe a placeholder is in the wrong place. Maybe the fixed text needs adjustment. Maybe a variable should be added or removed. The test phase reveals issues that planning alone cannot.

Step 5: Refine and Document

Based on the test phase, refine the template. Add usage notes describing when this template is the right choice and any tips for filling in the placeholders. Document any variations or extensions. The documentation makes the template usable by future you and by others on your team.

A Worked Example: Customer Reply Template

```
[Role] You are a customer support specialist for {{company_type}}.  [Context] A
customer has reached out with the following concern. {{customer_concern}}. Their
tone is {{customer_tone}}, and they appear to want {{customer_expectation}}.
[Instruction] Draft a reply that addresses the concern, sets appropriate
expectations, and ends on a constructive note.  [Constraints] Length: under
{{length}} words. Tone: {{response_tone}}. Do not: {{forbidden_elements}}.
[Output expectation] Format as a complete email with a subject line, greeting,
body in two paragraphs, a closing question if appropriate, and a signature line.
```

This template is filled in for each new task. The placeholders capture exactly what changes between customer replies, while the structure stays consistent. Filling in the template takes seconds. The output is reliably useful. After ten or twenty uses, you may notice patterns that suggest refinements, like adding a placeholder for resolution timeline or removing one that turned out to be unnecessary.

10.9 A Working Catalog of Common Templates

Beyond the customer reply template above, several common templates serve frequent business and creative tasks. The catalog below provides a starting set you can adapt.

Template: Meeting Summary

```
[Role] You are a careful note taker preparing meeting summaries for absent team
members.  [Context] The meeting was about {{meeting_topic}}. The attendees were
{{attendees}}.  [Source] Meeting transcript: {{transcript}}  [Instruction]
Produce a meeting summary highlighting decisions, action items, and unresolved
questions.  [Constraints] Length: under 200 words. Tone: factual and neutral. Do
not include side discussions that did not affect outcomes.  [Output expectation]
Produce three labeled sections: Decisions, Action Items (with owner and due date
when stated), and Open Questions.
```

Template: Code Review

```
[Role] You are a senior {{language}} engineer reviewing code for a
{{project_type}}.  [Context] The code below was written by a
{{author_seniority}} engineer for the purpose of {{code_purpose}}.  [Source]
Code: {{code}}  [Instruction] Review the code for correctness, robustness, and
readability. Identify the most important issues to fix.  [Constraints] Focus on
issues that affect correctness or robustness over stylistic preferences. Use
language a {{author_seniority}} engineer can follow.  [Output expectation]
Produce three labeled sections: Critical Issues (numbered list), Improvements
(numbered list), and Praise (one or two short statements about what is well
done).
```

Template: Analytical Memo

```
[Role] You are an analyst preparing a memo for {{audience}}.  [Context] The
analysis is about {{topic}}. The audience cares most about {{key_concerns}}.
[Source] Data: {{data}}  [Instruction] Produce an analytical memo identifying
the most important findings.  [Constraints] Length: roughly {{word_count}}
words. Tone: precise but accessible. Lead with the bottom line.  [Output
```

```
expectation] Format: Bottom line up front (one sentence), then three to five
short paragraphs each focused on one finding, then a concluding paragraph with
implications.
```

Template: Brainstorm

```
[Role] You are a {{role_type}} known for creative thinking.  [Context] The goal
is {{goal}}. Constraints include {{constraints}}.  [Instruction] Generate
{{count}} distinct ideas. Each should be genuinely different from the others,
not minor variations.  [Constraints] Keep each idea concise. Lean toward ideas
that play to {{strengths}}. Avoid {{forbidden_directions}}.  [Output
expectation] Produce a numbered list. For each idea, include a one sentence
pitch and a one sentence rationale.
```

Template: Onboarding Document

```
[Role] You are an experienced team lead writing onboarding documentation for new
hires.  [Context] The team is {{team_description}}. New hires typically have
{{prior_experience}}. The most common confusion in their first week is
{{common_confusion}}.  [Instruction] Produce a one page onboarding document that
helps a new hire orient themselves and start contributing.  [Constraints]
Length: under 500 words. Tone: warm and welcoming, not formal. Focus on what
they need to know in the first week, not eventually.  [Output expectation]
Produce four labeled sections: Welcome, How We Work, First Week Priorities, and
Where to Get Help.
```

10.10 Frameworks: A Closer Look

Section 10.2 introduced frameworks. This expansion looks at several specific frameworks in detail and discusses how to choose among them for different kinds of tasks.

The CRAFT Framework

CRAFT stands for Context, Role, Action, Format, Tone. It is a comprehensive framework that ensures the most important elements of a prompt are all included. Use it as a checklist for any non trivial prompt.

Element	What It Specifies	Example
Context	The situation and audience	We are launching a new feature to existing customers.

Element	What It Specifies	Example
Role	The AI's perspective	Act as a customer success manager.
Action	What the AI should do	Draft an email announcing the feature.
Format	The structure of the output	Email with subject line, three short paragraphs, sign off.
Tone	The voice of the output	Warm and informative, not pushy.

The TASK Framework

TASK stands for Topic, Audience, Style, Knowns. It is a lighter framework focused on the dimensions that most often change between similar prompts. Use it for everyday tasks where speed matters.

Element	What It Specifies	Example
Topic	What the prompt is about	Productivity tips for remote workers.
Audience	Who the output is for	Mid career professionals new to remote work.
Style	How the output should sound	Practical and accessible, not motivational.
Knowns	Facts the AI should rely on	Source material provided below.

The PARTS Framework

PARTS stands for Purpose, Audience, Role, Tone, Structure. It overlaps with CRAFT but emphasizes purpose explicitly, which keeps the prompt focused on outcomes.

Element	What It Specifies	Example
Purpose	Why the output is needed	To re engage customers who have not logged in recently.
Audience	Who will read the output	Trial users approaching the end of their free period.

Element	What It Specifies	Example
Role	The AI's perspective	Act as a friendly customer educator.
Tone	The emotional register	Helpful and confident, not desperate.
Structure	The shape of the output	Email with three short paragraphs and a clear call to action.

Choosing Among Frameworks

All of these frameworks are mnemonics for the same underlying ideas. Pick the one that fits your taste and the kinds of tasks you do most often. The point is not which framework you use but that you use one consistently. The framework forces you to think about all the dimensions, even the ones you might otherwise skip in haste.

10.11 Building a Personal Prompt Library: Practical Steps

Section 10.4 covered organizing prompt libraries. This expansion provides practical steps for actually building one, starting from nothing.

Step 1: Pick a Tool

Your library tool can be simple. A text document with named sections works fine for most people. A note taking app like Notion, Obsidian, or even Apple Notes works fine. A spreadsheet works fine. The tool matters less than the habit. Pick something you will actually use, not something you will admire and ignore.

Step 2: Start With Three Prompts

Identify three prompts you have written recently that produced excellent output. Save them in your library. Add a one line description of what each does. Add a one line description of when to use it. That is it. The library now exists. It is small, but it is real, and it can grow.

Step 3: Add the Save Habit

Every time a prompt produces excellent output, save it before moving on. The save takes seconds. The temptation is to skip it and move to the next task. Resist the temptation. Two weeks of consistent saving builds a library worth tens of hours of future time.

Step 4: Review Weekly

Once a week, spend five minutes reviewing your library. What new prompts did you add? Are any obsolete? Are any candidates for templating? Are there clusters of similar prompts that could become a single template? The review keeps the library alive and useful.

Step 5: Build Templates From Repeats

When you notice three or more similar prompts, build a template that captures the shared structure. Replace the three with the template plus a sample call. The library becomes more leveraged with each template.

Step 6: Tag and Categorize

As the library grows past twenty or so prompts, add tags or categories. By task type. By domain. By format. The tags make finding the right prompt faster than scrolling. The investment of tagging is small. The dividend is daily.

Step 7: Periodic Pruning

Once a quarter, look for prompts that are no longer useful. Templates that have been replaced. Patterns that no longer fit your work. Remove them. The library should serve you, not accumulate. Pruning keeps it sharp.

> **The Compounding Library**
>
> A library you build over a year holds the most useful patterns of your year. A library you build over five years holds the patterns of half a decade. The compounding effect of consistent saving is one of the most underrated benefits of working with AI seriously.

10.12 Scaling Across Teams

Section 10.5 introduced scaling prompting in workflows. This expansion looks at scaling beyond an individual to a team or organization, where the dynamics shift in important ways.

The Shared Library

A team can share a prompt library, just as it shares code, design assets, or documentation. The shared library has advantages over individual libraries. It captures the collective experience of many people. It reduces duplication of effort across team members. It produces consistent output across the team, which matters for customer facing or brand sensitive work. It accelerates onboarding of new team members, who can use proven prompts from day one.

Building a shared library requires a few practices. Someone needs to own it, even loosely, to ensure quality. Contributions need a light review process to keep the library coherent. Documentation needs to be consistent so prompts are findable and usable. Updates need to be communicated so the team knows when something has changed.

The Style Guide

Beyond individual prompts, teams benefit from a prompt style guide. The style guide captures the team's conventions for things like preferred tone, audience descriptions, format choices, and naming patterns. It is not a strict rulebook. It is a reference that aligns the team's prompting practice. New team members can read the style guide and produce output consistent with the team's voice quickly.

The Quality Standards

Teams that take prompting seriously develop quality standards for output. What makes a customer email acceptable? What makes a code review acceptable? What makes a research summary acceptable? The standards exist whether they are written down or not, but writing them down makes them shareable, debatable, and improvable. Standards plus a shared library plus a style guide together form a serious team prompting practice.

The Continuous Improvement Loop

Mature team practices include feedback loops. Output that does not meet quality standards becomes a learning opportunity. Why did the prompt not produce what was needed? What change to the prompt or template would have prevented the issue? The library improves over time as a result of these loops. Each problem becomes a contribution to the library, not just a frustration.

10.13 The Long View: Prompting as Profession

Prompting was not a profession five years ago. Today, prompt engineering is a recognized skill, and prompt engineers are sought after roles in many organizations. The question is not whether prompting will continue to be a valuable skill, but how it will continue to evolve.

How Prompting Skills Travel

The skills you build in prompting are portable. They transfer between AI tools. They transfer between domains. They transfer to communication with humans. They build clarity of thought, precision of expression, and the discipline of structured communication. These are universally valuable skills, and prompting is a particularly good way to develop them, because the AI's responses give you immediate feedback on the quality of your communication.

The Future of Prompting

AI tools will continue to evolve. Models will become more capable. Interfaces will change. Some of the specific techniques in this book may shift over time. The underlying principles, clarity, structure, audience awareness, iteration, will remain. The craft of communication endures. The tools change. Becoming someone who communicates well with AI prepares you to communicate well with whatever comes next.

Why This Matters

In an era when AI can produce so much so quickly, the bottleneck shifts. The bottleneck is no longer producing output. It is figuring out what output to produce, for whom, with what intent. That figuring out is the work that humans are still uniquely positioned to do. Prompting is the bridge between that human work and the AI's productive capacity. The better the bridge, the more productive the partnership.

> *Prompting is communication, communication is leadership, and leadership is the durable skill across every era of change. Building this craft is building yourself.*

10.14 Final Reflections and Where to Go Next

We have now covered the full territory of prompting from foundations to systems. Let us close with a few reflections that capture the spirit of what we hope you take from this book.

The Quiet Practice

Most of what makes a great prompt writer is invisible. It is the moment of pausing before sending. The mental checklist run quickly. The willingness to iterate when the first attempt is not quite right. The discipline of saving what works. The curiosity that asks why an output is off rather than simply moving on. None of these moments is dramatic. Together they compose a practice that produces consistently better work.

The Generosity of Specificity

Specificity in prompts is, in a deeper sense, an act of generosity toward your collaborator. You are providing the AI with what it needs to do its best work, rather than expecting it to read your mind. The same generosity transfers to working with humans. Specificity is care.

The Patience of Iteration

Iteration is not failure. It is craft. The most skilled communicators are not the ones who say everything perfectly the first time. They are the ones who know how to refine, adjust, and improve when the first attempt does not land. Patience with iteration is patience with the actual texture of communication, which is rarely a single perfect attempt and almost always a series of approximations.

The Joy of Mastery

There is a particular kind of satisfaction that comes from writing a prompt and getting back exactly what you wanted. The output lands. The work moves forward. The collaboration feels easy. This satisfaction grows with practice. It is one of the small pleasures of working seriously with AI tools, and it is available to everyone willing to invest in the craft.

Where to Go From Here

Five last suggestions before you close this book.

1. Tomorrow, write a prompt that uses every building block deliberately. Just one. Notice the difference.
2. Save your three best prompts from this week. Start your library.
3. Try one technique from this book that is new to you. Few shot. Multi step. Role assignment. Templates. Whichever feels most useful for your work.
4. Find one other person who works with AI seriously. Share what you have learned. Ask what they have learned. Cross pollination accelerates growth.
5. Stay curious. The field is young. The best practices are still being discovered. Be one of the people who discovers them.

Closing Note

Thank you for reading this book in full. The journey from understanding what a prompt is to building reusable prompt systems is significant. Whatever your starting point, you are now meaningfully further along than when you started. Use what you have learned. Build the library. Develop the practice. Communicate clearly with your AI collaborators. The craft is yours.

The end of one book is the beginning of the practice. Go build something good.

10.15 Building a Production Grade Prompt System

Beyond personal libraries, some teams build production grade prompt systems that operate at scale. These systems combine templates, frameworks, validation steps, monitoring, and continuous improvement into something that resembles infrastructure more than individual practice. Below is an overview of what production grade systems look like.

To close this book, here is a practice plan you can follow over the next 90 days to consolidate everything you have learned. The plan is structured but flexible. Adapt it to your situation. The point is the practice, not the specific schedule.

Days 1 to 7: Foundation

Reread chapters one and two. Pick three real tasks you have done recently and rewrite the prompts using the principles. Notice what you would do differently with what you now know.

Days 8 to 21: Construction

Spend two weeks deliberately practicing the four building blocks. For every important prompt, consciously include role, context, instruction, constraints, and output expectation. Notice when your output improves and when it does not. Save the prompts that produce excellent output.

Days 22 to 35: Patterns

Spend two weeks practicing design patterns. One day on direct prompts. One day on instruction based. One day on role based. One day on format driven. One day on multi step. Try each pattern on at least three real tasks.

Days 36 to 49: Techniques

Spend two weeks on core techniques. Practice few shot prompting deliberately. Practice step by step. Practice iterative prompting on a high stakes task that takes five or more rounds. Notice the rhythm of iteration.

Days 50 to 63: Optimization

Spend two weeks improving prompt quality. Audit your prompts for vague language. Practice tone control. Practice length specification. Practice the precision creativity balance. Notice the small improvements that compound into significant gains.

Days 64 to 77: Troubleshooting

Spend two weeks on diagnosis and recovery. When output disappoints, diagnose precisely before rewriting. Track which failure modes you encounter most. Develop personal repair habits for each.

Days 78 to 90: Systems

Spend the final two weeks building your library. Identify your most used prompts. Turn them into templates. Add tags and documentation. Set up a sustainable place to keep them. By the end of 90 days, you will have a working library that improves your daily AI work.

Beyond Day 90

After 90 days of structured practice, the habits will be yours. You will not need a plan to keep them. The practice will have become the way you work with AI. From there, your library will grow with each useful prompt you write. Your skills will deepen with each interesting task you encounter. The craft will be ongoing, but the foundation will be solid.

> **The 90 Day Investment**
>
> Three months of intentional practice is enough to transform your relationship with AI tools. Most people never make this investment, which is why most people remain stuck at casual or aware levels. The investment is small. The return is years of more effective work.

10.18 The Final Word

We have arrived at the last page of this book. Let us close with a single thought. The skills you have built reading and practicing this book are not just AI skills. They are communication skills. They are clarity of thought. They are the discipline of structured expression. They will serve you in conversations with humans as much as in conversations with AI.

In a world saturated with AI generated content, the people who matter most will be the people who can communicate clearly, who know what they want, who can articulate it precisely, and who can iterate when reality disagrees with their first draft. These are old skills, dressed in new tools. The tools will change. The skills will not.

Use what you have learned. Build the library. Develop the practice. Treat each prompt as an opportunity to be just a little clearer, a little more thoughtful, a little more specific than you would have been before reading this book. Over months and years, the small differences will compound into large ones.

> *The art of prompting is the art of communication, refined and made conscious. May the work you produce with AI reflect the clarity of your thinking, the depth of your craft, and the care you bring to your collaborators, both human and otherwise.*

Thank you for reading. The book ends here. The practice begins now. Go build something good.